Judith Wills

Virtually
Vegetarian

Judith Wills

Virtually Vegetarian

PIATKUS

First published in 1998 by
Judy Piatkus (Publishers) Ltd
5 Windmill Street, London W1P 1HF

The moral right of the author has been asserted

*A catalogue record for this book is available from
the British Library*

ISBN 0–7499–1812–8

Illustrations by Madeleine David
Photographs by Steve Baxter
Home economy by Jane Stevenson
Styling by Marian Price

Nutritional panels
researched by Gail Pollard, SRD, BSc

Typeset by Phoenix Photosetting, Chatham, Kent
Printed and bound in Great Britain by
Mackays of Chatham PLC, Chatham, Kent

CONTENTS

CHAPTER ONE

MEAT-FREE EATING FOR HEALTH

You don't have to be vegetarian to use the recipes in this book! In fact, although I hope that many vegetarians will enjoy most of the recipes it contains, I wrote *Virtually Vegetarian* for the growing band of people who are not *quite* vegetarian, but who have either stopped eating red meat altogether and eat mainly vegetarian foods (but also some fish, and maybe even a little poultry now and then), or who still eat red meat from time to time but are in desperate need of some new and healthy recipes for cooking without meat. If that sounds like you, you aren't alone. The growing band of 'demi-vegetarians' in the UK now numbers around 10 million, at the last estimate, and grows by about half a million a year. That's a very large number of people deciding to give red meat the thumbs-down.

Most people are making these changes for the sake of their health, and it is true that a diet that includes only a little meat can indeed be a very healthy one. In my view, demi-vegetarian eating combines the best of both the vegetarian and meat-eating worlds. In this chapter we will look at the reasons why a meat-free or low-meat diet can be so healthy and also examine any possible pitfalls. Finally, there's plenty of practical advice on using the recipes in this book within a healthy diet, and I've devised three sample diet plans for three different types of 'meat-free' eating to help you put it all together. And, for people who enjoy entertaining – and I think that's most of us! – there are some sample dinner-party menus, too.

WHY EAT LESS MEAT?

When most people in the UK talk about meat, they mean beef, lamb and pork, and for the purposes of this introductory chapter, this is also what I am referring to when I use the word 'meat'. Of the many people who no longer eat meat, some still eat poultry (usually organic poultry) and game, while others don't but still eat fish. The recipes in this book are based on vegetarian foods and fish, with an occasional recipe that can accommodate poultry if you would like it to.

There are many reasons why it might be a good idea to cut down on the amount of meat we eat, or even give it up altogether. Let's look at some of them:

✦ THE LINK BETWEEN A DIET HIGH IN MEAT AND AN INCREASED INCIDENCE OF CANCER

In autumn 1997, the World Cancer Research Fund published a report which said that up to 40 per cent of the world's cancers could be prevented by dietary changes alone, and it recommended a reduction in the consumption of red meat as one of the most important of those changes. In a separate study in 1997, the UK's Committee on the Medical Aspects of Food and Nutrition Policy (COMA) also recommended a cut in red meat consumption for anyone eating more than an average of 90 g a day – the amount of meat in, say, one small lamb chop – in order to reduce our high incidence of cancer. Cancers most strongly linked with red meat and saturated fat intake are breast cancer, bowel cancer, colon cancer and stomach cancer. Other research, in the USA, has also found that a diet high in red meat, especially well done red meat, increases the chance of getting stomach cancer by 100 per cent.

✦ THE LINK BETWEEN A HIGH-PROTEIN DIET AND OSTEOPOROSIS

In the UK (and other Western countries), we eat far more protein – found in concentrated amounts in red meat – than we need. It is now known that a diet that is so high in protein sets off a chain of reactions in the body which results in loss of calcium. As calcium loss from the bones is a major cause of osteoporosis, it is important to cut protein intake down to the recommended level (10–15 per cent of total daily calories). A vegetarian or demi-vegetarian diet is a simple way of achieving this.

✦ THE LINK BETWEEN SATURATED FAT AND CORONARY HEART DISEASE

This link is now established beyond doubt: a diet high in saturated fat is a strong contributory factor towards atherosclerosis (hardening of the arteries), coronary heart disease and stroke. One of the main sources of saturated fat in most Western people's diet is meat.

✦ THE COST OF GOOD-QUALITY RED MEAT

Since the BSE scandal, most people now realise that in order to give us low-cost meat over the past 20 years or so, meat producers have had to resort to intensive farming and rearing methods which are not always safe. Even if these methods don't bother you on health grounds, and if intensive farming is not something that worries you on compassionate grounds either, still the result has been too much meat that tastes of nothing and cooks badly. The fact is that meat reared by traditional or organic methods is the only meat really worth eating, the drawback being that such meat costs much more than factory-line meat, and all meat is expensive in terms of the world's ecology. A healthy vegetarian or demi-vegetarian diet is usually a much less expensive option in every way.

Why eat more non-meat meals?

Swapping to a demi-vegetarian diet doesn't just mean eating less, or no, meat; it also means eating *more* of other foods on a regular basis instead. This is where the real health benefits come in: you can eat *more* of all the many and varied foods which not only offer good, basic nutrition, but also actually offer you health protection in other ways, too. Let's look at some of those ways:

✦ A DIET HIGH IN FRUITS, VEGETABLES AND HIGH-FIBRE CARBOHYDRATE FOODS (SUCH AS WHOLE GRAINS AND PULSES) HELPS TO PROTECT AGAINST MANY DISEASES AND HEALTH PROBLEMS

We now know that eating plenty of fruits and vegetables is one of the best ways to protect ourselves from many different types of cancer, including cancers of the lung, mouth, bladder and stomach. That is why the World Health Organisation, the World Cancer Research Fund and the UK Department of Health all recommend that we eat at least five portions of fruit and vegetables every day. It is thought that fruits and vegetables work to protect us against cancer in various ways: they are high in anti-oxidant vitamin C, which may help to 'fight off' cancer cells; they are high in fibre, which is also linked to cancer protection; many are rich in carotenoids, which may help boost the immune system.

Fruits and vegetables also protect against heart disease; several recent studies show that the higher the intake of fruits and vegetables, the lower the incidence of deaths from cardiovascular disease, heart attack and stroke. A high fruit and vegetable diet is also related to a more general decrease in mortality from all causes.

Other health problems, such as diabetes, obesity and high blood pressure, have also been shown to occur much less often in populations with a high intake of fruits and vegetables, and a 1997 study of children associated a high intake of fruits and vegetables with improved lung function and less wheezing as in, say, asthma and bronchitis.

It's a similar story for diets high in other plant foods, such as pulses, grains, nuts and seeds. The insoluble fibre content of these foods is thought to help prevent diseases of the digestive tract, such as bowel, colon and stomach cancer, diverticular disease, and more common problems such as constipation.

The soluble fibre content of foods such as oats and pulses is known to help lower blood cholesterol and thus protect against heart disease.

✦ A HEALTHY VEGETARIAN OR DEMI-VEGETARIAN DIET HELPS YOU TO CONTROL YOUR WEIGHT

All research shows that people who eat a low-meat or meat-free diet are, on average, thinner than others and find it easier to maintain their weight below the upper limits for desirable weight set by the UK Department of Health. This is probably at least partly because vegetarian and demi-vegetarian diets tend to be higher in foods that have a high bulk but low density and low calorific and fat value, such as fruits, vegetables and grains. Moreover, non-meat sources of protein, such as pulses, white fish and tofu, tend to be lower in fat and calories than meat sources of protein.

✦ A DIET RICH IN FISH, PARTICULARLY OILY FISH, HELPS TO PROTECT AGAINST HEART DISEASE, STROKE AND SOME CANCERS

When eaten regularly, Omega-3 fatty acids, found in many types of fish, including salmon, trout, herring, sardines, mackerel, tuna and others, help to lower blood cholesterol levels and also offer protection against atherosclerosis and stroke. There is strong evidence to show that eating oily fish regularly also helps to protect against some cancers, including breast, prostate and bowel cancer, by acting as an anti-inflammatory agent.

Apart from its obvious nutritional benefits as an excellent source of low-fat protein, the positive health protection that fish offers is a good reason why a demi-vegetarian diet might actually be better for you than a completely vegetarian diet. However, if you don't eat fish, you can replace the Omega-3 fatty acids in your diet with a daily dose of linseed (flax) oil, available from health food shops. It is one of the few plant foods that contain high amounts of the beneficial Omega-3s.

ACHIEVING A BALANCED DIET WITHOUT MEAT

When people want to reduce the amount of meat in their diets, or cut it out altogether, they often worry that they will miss out on vital nutrients, or cause other problems. Here we look at the most frequent questions I am asked:

✦ WITHOUT MEAT, HOW WILL I GET THE IRON I NEED?

Red meat is a good source of iron but, as you will see from the chart opposite, it is by no means the only source. Problems only arise when people give up meat and don't take care to include a good variety of other iron-rich foods in their diet. As I always say, any diet, whatever types of food it contains, has to be balanced and varied to be nutritionally successful. A diet that includes plenty of dark leafy greens, pulses and whole grains should not be short of iron, and plenty of breakfast cereals are now fortified with iron, too. One good tip is always to eat iron-rich foods with a vitamin C-rich food, as the vitamin C aids iron absorption.

SOURCES OF IRON IN A NON-MEAT DIET

(The estimated average daily requirement for females aged 15–50 is 11.4 mg; for males aged 19–50 it is 8.7 mg.)

Food	Amount of iron in mg per 100 g of food
Dulse (seaweed)	150.0
Curry powder	30.0
Bran flakes	20.0
Molasses	15.0
Pistachio nuts	14.0
Alfalfa sprouts	13.0
Chinese mushrooms	12.0
Wheatgerm	8.5
Soya beans	8.4
Sesame seeds	7.8
Lentils	7.6
Wholewheat breakfast biscuits	7.5
Dried peaches	6.8
Kidney beans	6.7
Black-eye beans	6.5
Chick peas	6.4
Egg yolk	6.1
Pot barley	6.0
Butter beans	6.0
Tofu	5.2
Bulghar wheat	5.0
Brazil nuts	4.2
Broad beans	4.2
Dried apricots	4.1
Wholemeal bread	2.7
Peas	1.9
Spinach	1.6
Broccoli	1.1

(This chart isn't comprehensive as I've only included some of the more popular vegetarian foods; many other foods have good amounts of iron in them, including wholemeal flour, spaghetti, other pulses, nuts and seeds, other vegetables, other breakfast cereals, and so on. But you can see that iron isn't difficult to come by if you eat a varied diet, not forgetting plenty of vitamin C at each meal.)

✦ WITHOUT MEAT, HOW WILL I GET VITAMIN B₁₂ IN MY DIET?

There is no problem with this unless you decide to become vegan – that is, to eat no meat, fish, poultry or dairy produce of any kind. Vitamin B_{12} is only found naturally in these foods; many vegans take a B_{12} supplement or use B_{12} fortified soya milk.

✦ IF I REPLACE MEAT IN MY DIET WITH MORE DAIRY PRODUCE, FOR PROTEIN, WON'T I STILL BE EATING TOO MUCH SATURATED FAT?

Probably. If you are giving up or cutting back on meat for health reasons, because of its saturated fat content, the worst thing you can do is to start eating extra full-fat dairy produce instead, as you will more than likely be eating *more* saturated fat, rather than less. Full-fat milk, cheeses such as Stilton, Cheddar and other hard cheeses and cream cheeses, are high-fat foods. If you are eating less meat and more cheese for health reasons alone, then my advice would be to go back to eating a little meat – lean, lightly cooked organic meat. Alternatively (and much more beneficial), learn how to eat a tasty, varied, balanced diet which doesn't rely too heavily on high-fat dairy produce.

The recipes and diet plans in this book will give you plenty of ideas for healthier eating, and the fat content of every recipe is provided to help you keep your fat intake within sensible limits. (The chart below shows what daily fat intake you should aim for.) My recipes are not ultra-low in total fat (because the unsaturated fats can be very good for you and we all need some fat in our diets), but they are low in saturated fat because they make full use of pulses, tofu, Quorn (see page 105), fish, low-fat dairy produce and other healthier sources of protein. As I said earlier in this chapter, we nearly all eat much more protein than we need for good health anyway. Learn to cook with more plant foods and that way you will also get the added bonus of extra fibre in your diet – something dairy produce doesn't contain at all.

MAXIMUM DAILY RECOMMENDED FAT INTAKES

	Total Fat*	Saturated Fat**
Women		
On weight maintenance diet of 1,900 calories a day	63 g	21 g
On slimming diet of 1,300 calories a day	56 g	14 g
Men		
On weight maintenance diet of 2,500 calories a day	83 g	27 g
On slimming diet of 1,600 calories a day	53 g	17 g

* Based on 30% of total daily calorie intake as fat
** Based on 10% of total daily calorie intake as saturated fat
(Both these percentages are as recommended by major health organisations.)

✦ ISN'T IT TRUE THAT THE PROTEIN FOUND IN PLANTS IS OF INFERIOR QUALITY TO THAT FOUND IN MEAT?

Animal protein is sometimes called 'first class' protein because it contains all eight of the amino acids that form a complete protein food. The only plant food containing all eight together is soya, which is also therefore a 'first class' protein. However, you don't need all eight amino acids together in one food to get good-quality protein in a meal. The easiest way to ensure this is to mix plant protein foods that 'complement' each other and provide, between them, all the amino acids you need. This is achieved by mixing pulses with grains (as in beans on toast or hummus and pitta bread, or a salad of brown rice and kidney beans, and so on) or pulses with nuts and seeds. However, many experts now believe that as long as your diet is varied you needn't worry too much about combining your protein foods is such a way at every meal. And, of course, for demi-vegetarians, fish is a complete protein, as is the protein in dairy produce and eggs, so it is really only vegans who need be careful about their protein intake, which is why tofu (made from soya beans) is such a good food for them.

TOP TEN TIPS FOR HEALTHY EATING WITHOUT MEAT

1. Get a wide and varied diet.
2. Don't rely too heavily on dairy produce in your meals, particularly full-fat dairy produce.
3. Eat plenty of fresh fruits, and dried fruits in moderation too.
4. Eat plenty of fresh vegetables.
5. Eat plenty of starchy 'complex carbohydrate' foods such as bread, potatoes, pasta, rice and barley.
6. Choose whole grain versions of foods at least some of the time, e.g. wholemeal bread, wholewheat pasta, brown rice and pot barley. These contain more B vitamins and fibre than the refined white versions.
7. Eat pulses regularly.
8. If you eat fish, eat plenty of oily fish as well as white fish.
9. Cook your food by healthy methods, using saturated fats such as butter only in moderation. Pure vegetable oils, such as olive oil, corn oil, sunflower oil, groundnut oil and safflower oil, contain a high percentage of the healthy unsaturated fats.
10. Choose the best-quality ingredients and foods you can; when choosing fruit, vegetables and so on, buy organic if possible. These will be free of pesticide and other residues, and also often have a much better flavour.

SLIMMING SENSE

It is estimated that around a third of the UK population is overweight and that around one in ten people are clinically obese, i.e. *very* overweight. It might be that you need to lose some weight, and perhaps you have been attracted to this book because you think that meals without meat might help.

As explained above, vegetarians and vegans do seem to stay slimmer than meat eaters. By following the general guidelines in this book and by using my recipes, none of which are very high in calories or fat, you might find you slowly lose weight quite naturally without having to go on 'a diet' as such. I hope that you do and I think that you will. The diet plans given on pages 9–16 are for weight maintenance or slimming; if you are trying to lose weight, simply follow the guidelines given below.

Here are a few helpful hints for demi-vegetarians trying to lose weight:

+ High-fat foods also usually contain a lot of calories. Although foods high in unsaturated fats can be good for your health, you may restrict them slightly more than someone on a weight maintenance diet. The foods high in unsaturated fats include: all vegetable oils, avocados, nuts and seeds.

+ The high-fat foods definitely to try to cut right down on are full-fat dairy produce such as hard and cream cheeses, full-fat milk and cream. Most bought products, such as cakes, biscuits, pastries and desserts, are high in fat and calories, so choose fruit, dried fruit, crudités and other low-fat natural foods for between-meals snacks and desserts (or use my recipes for desserts).

+ Exercise a little portion control and give yourself slightly smaller helpings at every meal. If you still feel hungry five minutes after you have finished eating, you could have a little more. It is too easy to get in the habit of eating more than you need to satisfy your hunger. If using the recipes in this book, have a full portion, but cut down a little on extras, especially fatty extras.

+ Cut down on alcohol. A little alcohol, particularly red wines and dark beers, can be good for you, but alcohol contains quite a few calories and it is easy to get through more than you realise. By cutting back on, say, half a bottle of wine a day, you could lose over half a pound a week even if you altered your diet in no other way! And if you have been drinking too much you will be doing your health a favour in other ways, too.

+ Take more regular exercise, particularly the kind that gets your heart working harder, such as brisk walking or cycle riding. Exercise burns off calories and helps to speed up your metabolic rate.

+ Don't try to 'crash' diet – long-term, anyone who restricts calories too much has more chance of failing than someone prepared to lose weight slowly.

THE DIET PLANS

The diet plans on the following pages are blueprints to help you plan your own healthy eating. Eaten exactly as laid out, they each contain approximately 1,600 calories a day.

ADJUSTING THE PLANS TO YOUR NEEDS

A daily intake of 1,600 calories is suitable for a MALE who is trying to lose weight. A MALE *not* trying to lose weight should add extra food to the meals listed in the form of extra healthy between-meals snacks, maybe a glass of beer or wine, and perhaps slightly larger portions of bread where mentioned.

A FEMALE not trying to lose weight should add a little extra food to the meals listed, perhaps with one extra daily snack and a glass of wine, or a little extra bread and vegetables. A FEMALE trying to lose weight should cut the calories in the given plans a little by replacing some of the higher-calorie main meal suggestions with lower-calorie dishes from the recipes in this book (a browse through will soon give you plenty of ideas) and by cutting out the daily treat.

RECIPES
In all the diet plans, recipes for the dishes printed in *italics* can be found in this book – see the index for page numbers.

THE DEMI-VEGETARIAN PLAN (INCLUDES FISH)

Read the notes above, then follow the plan as laid out, choosing one of the breakfasts every day plus EXTRAS – 250 ml (8 fl oz) skimmed milk for use in drinks or on its own, and a DAILY TREAT of either any chocolate bar containing no more than 100 calories, 1 glass of wine or 300 ml (½ pint) beer, or two digestive biscuits.

Breakfasts   Choose one of the following for breakfast each day, varying your choice if possible.

✦ 4 tablespoons natural low-fat bio yogurt with 1 portion fresh fruit chopped in and 1 teaspoon sesame seeds sprinkled over PLUS 1 medium slice wholemeal bread with a little sunflower spread and yeast extract or pure fruit spread.

✦ Medium bowl no-added-sugar muesli with 1 portion fresh fruit chopped in served with 125 ml (4 fl oz) skimmed or semi-skimmed milk.

✦ Fresh orange juice; 2 wholewheat breakfast biscuits with 150 ml (¼ pint) skimmed or semi-skimmed milk and a little brown sugar, PLUS 1 piece of fresh fruit.

DAY ONE
Lunch
Saffron Fish Soup
1 crusty bread roll
Mixed salad

1 apple or orange

Evening Meal
Spaghetti with Anchovies and Fried Herb Breadcrumbs
Green salad

1 banana

DAY TWO
Lunch
1 wholemeal pitta bread filled with 1 hard-boiled egg, chopped and mixed with salad items of choice plus low-fat mayonnaise

1 orange or 2 kiwi fruits

Evening Meal
Chinese-Style Steamed Tilapia
Broccoli
Egg thread noodles
Blackberry and Apple Layers

DAY THREE
Lunch
Tuna Pâté with three dark rye crispbreads
250 ml (8 fl oz) fresh chilled ready-made vegetable soup, heated
4 tablespoons natural low-fat bio yogurt mixed with 1 medium chopped banana

Evening Meal
Jambalaya
Green salad
Mixed Fruits en Papillote

DAY FOUR
Lunch
Sandwich of two slices of rye bread lightly spread with sunflower spread and filled with 50 g (2 oz) medium-fat cheese (such as feta or Brie) plus salad items of choice and a spoonful of *Pineapple Coleslaw*
Fresh Tomato and Basil Soup

1 satsuma

Evening Meal
Bean and Pasta Bake
2 portions green vegetables of choice

1 banana

DAY FIVE
Lunch
Smoked Mackerel Salad
1 slice rye bread

1 satsuma

Evening Meal
Stir-Fried Peppers with Rosti and Poached Eggs
Crunchy Pear Sundaes

DAY SIX
Lunch
Twice-Baked Potatoes
Salad of sliced tomato and cucumber

1 apple

Evening Meal
Garlic and Chilli Scampi with Avocado
Mixed leaf salad
Zabaglione with Summer Fruits

DAY SEVEN
Lunch
Spanish Omelette
1 good slice crusty bread
Large mixed salad

Evening Meal
Lentil and Roasted Squash Gratin
2 portions green vegetables of choice
Old-Fashioned Baked Apples

DRINKS

Drink plenty of water, well-diluted fresh fruit juices or vegetable juices, weak green or black tea and coffee in addition to your chosen diet plan.

THE VEGETARIAN PLAN (NO FISH, INCLUDES DAIRY PRODUCE)
Read the notes on page 9, then follow the plan as laid out, choosing one of
the breakfasts every day plus EXTRAS – 250 ml (8 fl oz) skimmed milk for use
in drinks or on its own, and a DAILY TREAT of any chocolate bar containing no
more than 100 calories, 1 glass of wine or 300 ml (½ pint) beer, or two
digestive biscuits.

Breakfasts   Choose one of the following for breakfast each day, varying
your choice if possible.

✦ 2 shredded wholewheat breakfast biscuits with 125 ml (4 fl oz) skimmed
   milk and a little brown sugar PLUS 1 slice wholemeal bread with a little
   sunflower spread and low-sugar jam or marmalade.

✦ 200 g (7 oz) natural low-fat bio yogurt topped with 1 portion chopped
   fresh fruit of choice and 1 handful no-added-sugar muesli; glass of fresh
   orange juice.

✦ Medium bowl porridge made with traditional (not quick cook) oats and
   skimmed milk/water, topped with a little runny honey and 100 ml (3½ fl
   oz) skimmed milk PLUS 1 slice wholemeal bread with a little sunflower
   spread and yeast extract.

DAY ONE
Lunch
Italian Pasta and Vegetable Soup
1 *ciabatta* roll
1 banana

Evening Meal
Lentil Pie with Parsnip, Leek and Potato Topping
Broccoli and peas
Old-Fashioned Baked Apples
2 tablespoons low-fat custard

DAY TWO
Lunch
Feta and Watercress Pâté
2 slices wholemeal bread
250 ml (8 fl oz) fresh chilled vegetable soup, heated
Mixed salad

Evening Meal
Curried Potatoes and Spinach
Spiced Couscous
1 apple or orange

DAY THREE

Lunch
Unusual Scrambled Eggs
1 banana
1 nectarine or kiwi fruit

Evening Meal
Pasta Primavera
Large mixed green salad
Peach Melba Meringue Nests

DAY FOUR

Lunch
Garlic, Pea and Potato Soup
50 g (2 oz) bread roll
Fresh fruit salad topped with 2 tablespoons natural 8%-fat fromage frais

Evening Meal
Gratin of Polenta and Mediterranean Vegetables
Pear and Plum Pudding

DAY FIVE

Lunch
Pan-Cooked Pizza
Pineapple Coleslaw
1 apple

Evening Meal
Chilli Beans with Tortilla Crust
Herb Salad with Orange Vinaigrette
1 low-fat bio fruit yogurt

DAY SIX

Lunch
Fruit and Nut Rice
1 piece fresh fruit of choice

Evening Meal
Spinach and Ricotta Lasagne
Large mixed salad
1 x 100 ml (3½ fl oz) individual tub good-quality vanilla ice cream

Day seven
Lunch
Tabbouleh with Grilled Halloumi

1 banana

Evening Meal
Aubergine and Lentil Gratin
2 portions green vegetables of choice
1 medium portion new potatoes

1 apple or orange

THE DAIRY-FREE PLAN

This plan is suitable for both vegans and fish eaters who eat no dairy produce. If you are a vegan who eats no dairy produce, simply follow the diet as laid out. For those who eat fish but no dairy, an optional fish dish has been suggested on a few of the days. Choose this instead of the vegan option if you wish.

Either way, read the notes on page 9, then follow the plan as laid out, choosing one of the breakfasts every day plus EXTRAS – 250 ml (8 fl oz) soya milk (see note in box) for use in drinks or on its own, and a DAILY TREAT of 1 glass of wine, 300 ml (½ pint) beer or 1 apple and date dessert bar (from a health food shop).

SOYA MILK
Anyone worried about osteoporosis should choose soya milk fortified with calcium; for vegans it is also wise to choose soya milk fortified with vitamin B_{12}.

Breakfasts   Choose one of the following for breakfast each day, varying your choice if possible.

+ 4 tablespoons natural soya yogurt with 1 portion fresh fruit chopped in PLUS 1 slice organic wholemeal bread with a little soya margarine and pure fruit spread.

+ Medium bowl no-added-sugar muesli with fresh orange juice poured over to taste, with 1 portion fresh berry fruits or 1 chopped orange and 2 teaspoons chopped hazelnuts.

+ Medium portion baked beans in tomato sauce on 1 slice rye bread with a little soya margarine; 1 large glass of fresh orange juice.

DAY ONE

Lunch
Lentil, Squash and Carrot Soup
Wholemeal roll and soya margarine

1 banana

Evening Meal
Pasta with Storecupboard Sauce
Large mixed salad

Fresh Figs in Red Wine

DAY TWO

Lunch
Spinach, Chick Peas and Peppers
1 naan bread, warmed in the oven

1 orange

Evening Meal
Jambalaya
Large mixed salad

Fresh fruit salad

DAY THREE

Lunch
Avocado Salad
Large slice rye bread
50 g (2 oz) walnuts

Evening Meal
Bean and Tomato Hotpot
1 portion dark green cabbage
1 portion broccoli

1 banana

DAY FOUR

Lunch
Fresh Tomato and Basil Soup
Mr Herbert's Baked Potatoes
Green salad

Evening Meal
Ragu of Brown Lentils served on 1 portion wholewheat spaghetti
Tomato and cucumber salad
or
Swordfish, Potato and Olive Gratin served with *Sautéed Spinach and Pine Nuts*

1 piece fresh fruit of choice

Day five
Lunch
Fruit and Nut Rice (made with soya yogurt instead of dairy yogurt)
1 orange

Evening Meal
Pappardelle with Peppers
Large mixed salad
Peach Melba Meringue Nests (made using soya ice cream)

Day six
Lunch
1 wholemeal pitta bread filled with hummus and mixed salad
or
Smoked Mackerel Salad plus 3 rye crispbreads
1 banana

Evening Meal
Lentil and Sweet Potato Curry
1 portion brown rice or *Spiced Couscous*
Mixed Fruits en Papillote

Day seven
Lunch
Italian Pasta and Vegetable Soup
1 *ciabatta* roll
1 apple

Evening Meal
Vegetable Biryani
or
Grilled Salmon with a Lentil Salsa
New potatoes
Broccoli
Old-fashioned Baked Apples

MENUS FOR ENTERTAINING

If you've invited friends or family to supper, and need some menu ideas, you'll find plenty of recipes in this book to help you produce a memorable, tasty and satisfying meal. Try some of the suggestions below for balanced, three-course dinners. Page numbers for all the recipes can be found in the index.

FRENCH-STYLE

Saffron Fish Soup
Provençal Tuna Steaks au Gratin or *Mushroom Crêpes*
Filo Strawberry Cups

BRITISH-STYLE

Broccoli Soup
Creamy Vegetable Pie or *Traditional Fish Pie*
Crunchy Pear Sundaes

ITALIAN-STYLE

Crostini with Red Peppers
Fusilli with Salmon and Leek or *Spinach and Pine Nut Risotto*
Zabaglione with Summer Fruits

EAST MEDITERRANEAN-STYLE

Crumble-Topped Aubergines
Coulibiac Filo Tarts or *Stuffed Vine Leaves with Egg and Lemon Sauce*
Fresh Figs in Red Wine

INDIAN-STYLE

Chapati with *Tzatziki*
Tomato and onion salad
Vegetable Biryani
Mixed Fruits en Papillote

SPANISH-STYLE

Salad of Artichoke Hearts and Asparagus
Shellfish Paella
Baked Peaches Amaretti

ORIENTAL-STYLE

Mushroom and Sweetcorn Sizzle with Thai Flavours
Stir-Fried Squid and Vegetables
Chinese-style Rice and Eggs
Fresh lychees

NUTRITION NOTES

To help you work out a healthy balanced diet, nutrition notes are provided with all the recipes in the following chapters. The figures given are per portion.

Calorie and fat counts are self-explanatory. Follow the guidelines for maximum intake outlined on pages 6 and 9.

Protein content is given as High, Medium or Low. High means that the recipe provides over 15 per cent of its calories as protein; Medium means that 10–15 per cent of the calories are protein; Low means that less than 10 per cent of the calories are protein.

Carbohydrate content is star rated. ★ means that less than 35 per cent of the calories provided by the dish are carbohydrate; ★★ means that 36–50 per cent of the calories are carbohydrate; ★★★ means that over 50 per cent of the calories are carbohydrate. (The UK Department of Health recommends that at least 50 per cent of daily calorie intake should come from carbohydrate.)

Fibre content is given in grams per portion. The Department of Health recommends that everybody should have an average daily intake of 18 g fibre.

CHAPTER TWO

SOUPS AND STARTERS

Home-made soup is the most underrated food ever. I'm not at all sure how I would have managed my culinary life to date – feeding ravenous children, a hungry husband or unexpected guests; using up garden gluts; packing winter lunchboxes; loading up the freezer – without it. Filling, light, hot, cold, quick, slow, spicy, bland, smooth, chunky – whatever you want soup to be, it can be; it is so versatile that you could cook a soup every day of the year and not repeat yourself. Even more important, most soup recipes are easy (if not always quick) and very forgiving; soup-making is rarely an exact science, and for that I and busy working parents everywhere should be very grateful. Children love most soups and even those who won't eat vegetables when served as a side dish will eat them in soup form. Moreover, although soup *can* be expensive, most soups are not.

However, the main benefits of home-made soup, for our purposes, are these: (i) soup is an ideal vehicle for getting more fresh vegetables and pulses into your diet in a delicious way; (ii) if you have an electric blender in the kitchen (my one and only truly indispensable electric kitchen gadget, apart from the kettle), you can make rich, creamy-tasting soup concoctions without lots of extra fat and – if you're watching your weight – calories; (iii) when you make soup you retain all the goodness of your ingredients (unlike, for example, when you boil vegetables and throw half the water-soluble vitamins down the drain with the cooking water).

My advice, therefore, is to start making your own soups and do your health, your purse and your time a favour. Use the small selection of soups in this chapter as inspiration for your own inventions. The most simple and quick soups – made by just simmering a selection of vegetables in a good stock, and then puréeing and seasoning – are fresh, tasty and wholesome. Storecupboard items, such as dried mushrooms, lentils, split peas and grains, can be used to bulk out soups and add nutrients. A spoonful of sundried tomato paste, pesto or tapenade can do wonders for a bland soup and, if you can be bothered, a garnish of fresh herbs makes a great finishing touch.

Light soups make ideal starters but many are too heavy to be a good first course when you're entertaining, so I've included some easy and light starters in this chapter. All the starters would also make a very light lunchtime snack – or even a substantial lunch if you increase portion sizes – and they would certainly be good mixed and matched as party buffet items.

When considering first courses for your own supper parties, bear in mind the balance of the meal. Only one of the three courses should be rich or substantial, and no more than two should contain similar ingredients; if your main course has a cheese sauce, don't choose, for example, Feta and Watercress Pâté (page 30) for your starter.

Starters, like soups, can be an ideal opportunity to enjoy vegetables, but if you haven't time to make an elaborate starter, or even a dip or pâté, it doesn't matter. Just serve some tender fresh vegetables in season, roasted – for example, asparagus brushed with olive oil, roasted, and then served with Parmesan shavings. Alternatively, serve a perfect, orange-fleshed ripe melon (full of the anti-oxidant beta-carotene, which helps protect against heart disease and other health problems) sprinkled with a little balsamic vinegar; or try a creamy avocado (rich in vitamin E), sliced and topped with a vinaigrette dressing spiced with a spoonful of chilli sauce; or how about a quick salad, made using a pack of mixed ready-washed leaves and a jar of drained artichoke hearts; or a selection of crudités with a quick dip of Greek yogurt, crushed garlic and diced cucumber . . . The possibilities are endless!

Broccoli Soup

<u>SERVES 4</u>

CALORIES: 175	PROTEIN: HIGH
TOTAL FAT: 5.6 g	CARBOHYDRATE: ★★
SATURATED FAT: 2.9 g	FIBRE: 4 g

BROCCOLI is one of those amazing superfoods that we now know we should all eat on a regular basis because of the fine array of nutrients and anti-cancer 'secret agents' it contains. Here's what to make when broccoli boredom sets in.

1 medium mild onion, finely chopped	300 ml (½ pint) semi-skimmed milk
1 large old potato, peeled and chopped	salt and black pepper
500 ml (18 fl oz) good-quality vegetable stock	2 tablespoons half-fat crème fraîche
400 g (14 oz) good fresh broccoli, cut into florets	

Put the onion, potato and stock in a saucepan, stir and bring to a simmer. Simmer gently for 30 minutes or until the vegetables are tender, then add the broccoli and simmer for a further few minutes until it is just tender. Remove from the heat and leave to cool slightly.

Pour the contents of the saucepan into an electric blender and purée until smooth. Add the milk and blend again for a few seconds. Return the soup to the saucepan, season and bring to a simmer. Serve with the crème fraîche swirled in.

NOTES AND TIPS
✦ *You can make a similar soup using cauliflower instead of broccoli. Cauliflower is also an excellent vegetable though it contains much less beta-carotene than broccoli.*
✦ *Frozen broccoli would be almost as good as fresh in this soup.*

Fresh Tomato and Basil Soup

SERVES 4

CALORIES: 84	PROTEIN: HIGH
TOTAL FAT: 2.6 g	CARBOHYDRATE: ★★★
SATURATED FAT: 0.3 g	FIBRE: 3.3 g

DON'T bother making this soup with those insipid, tough, half-ripe tomatoes; wait for late summer when you can get juicy, tasty tomatoes in season and at low cost.

450 g (1 lb) good tomatoes, skinned and chopped (see Note, below)	2 large spring onions, chopped
	500 ml (18 fl oz) passata
1 tablespoon sundried tomato paste	salt and black pepper
1 good-quality unsalted vegetable stock cube	2 tablespoons chopped fresh basil

Put the tomatoes, tomato paste, stock cube, onions and a little of the passata into an electric blender and blend for a few seconds until you have a rough purée. Tip the purée into a saucepan and add the rest of the passata. Season and stir, then heat gently for a few minutes, adding the basil for the last minute of cooking. Check the seasoning and serve.

NOTES AND TIPS
✦ *This soup is meant to be light and fresh. It is also nice served chilled on a hot day.*
✦ *To skin tomatoes, make a cross in their stalk ends and blanch in boiling water for 30 seconds. Drain and, when cooled a little, peel off the skins. You can, if you like, also de-seed the tomatoes by halving them and squeezing out the pips, but I don't usually bother with this.*

Italian Pasta and Vegetable Soup

<u>SERVES 4</u>

CALORIES: 230	PROTEIN: HIGH
TOTAL FAT: 7.6 g	CARBOHYDRATE: ★★★
SATURATED FAT: 1.5 g	FIBRE: 6.3 g

THIS is an excellent lunch soup when you feel like something filling and tasty yet highly nutritious. All you need do is chop a few vegetables and it more or less cooks itself.

1 tablespoon olive oil	1 × 400 g (14 oz) can mixed beans (not chick
1 large leek, thinly sliced	peas), well rinsed and drained
1 large or 2 small carrots, diced	1 rounded tablespoon chilled ready-made pesto
2 medium tomatoes, chopped	salt and black pepper
1 medium courgette, chopped	chopped fresh flat-leaved parsley or basil to garnish
1 litre (2 pints) good vegetable stock	(optional)
60 g (2½ oz) small pasta shapes	

Heat the oil in a large saucepan, add the leek and carrot, and cook, stirring, for 1 minute. Add the tomatoes, courgette, stock, pasta and beans, cover, and simmer for 30 minutes. When everything is tender, stir in the pesto. Add black pepper and a little salt if you think the soup needs it. Serve immediately, garnished with flat-leaved parsley or basil if you have it.

NOTES AND TIPS

✦ *If you want to make your own fresh pesto you can, of course, by pounding (using a pestle and mortar) some fresh leafy green herbs (basil and/or flat-leaved parsley are ideal) with garlic, salt, pine nuts and olive oil.*

✦ *This soup is nice with some grated Pecorino or Parmesan cheese sprinkled over, which would add approximately 30 calories and 2.2 g of fat per tablespoon of cheese.*

Saffron Fish Soup

SERVES 4

CALORIES: 314	PROTEIN: HIGH
TOTAL FAT: 15 g	CARBOHYDRATE: ★
SATURATED FAT: 2.4 g	FIBRE: 2.4 g

ONE of the nice things about fish soup is that you can use whichever type of fish looks freshest and best at your fish counter.

1 tablespoon light olive oil	1 × 400 g (14 oz) can Italian plum tomatoes
1 medium mild onion, finely chopped	800 ml (28 fl oz) fresh fish stock (see Note, below)
2 cloves garlic, crushed	1 sachet saffron strands
2 sticks celery, chopped	800 g (1¾ lb) fillets of fish, at least two kinds, e.g.
1 bulb fennel, sliced (see Note, below)	cod, salmon, monkfish, red mullet (but not
1 teaspoon chopped fresh thyme or dill	smoked fish), skinned and cut into pieces
juice of ½ lemon	

Heat the oil in a large frying pan, add the onion, garlic, celery and fennel, and cook, stirring, until soft. Add the remaining ingredients, except the fish, to the pan and simmer for a few minutes until the vegetables are tender to the bite. Add the fish and simmer gently, uncovered, for a few more minutes until the fish is cooked (don't overcook). Serve immediately.

NOTES AND TIPS
✦ *Serve with some Italian bread.*
✦ *You can get fish stock in most supermarkets now, but if you want to make your own, buy the fish on the bone and fillet it yourself, or ask your fishmonger for a 'bag of bones'. Simmer the bones and fish trimmings with water, leek, carrot, celery and a bouquet garni for 40 minutes, then strain.*
✦ *If you can't get a bulb of fennel, don't worry; use an extra stick of celery plus a teaspoon of crushed fennel seeds instead.*

Garlic, Pea and Potato Soup

<u>SERVES 4</u>

CALORIES: 215	PROTEIN: HIGH
TOTAL FAT: 4.4 g	CARBOHYDRATE: ★★★
SATURATED FAT: 0.6 g	FIBRE: 6.9 g

I SUPPOSE there are still some people around who don't like garlic but I think the numbers are diminishing! As you will no doubt know by now, when garlic is cooked it loses its strong, raw taste, and when it is roasted, as it is in this soup, it is loveliest of all! It is also an excellent anti-oxidant and antiseptic.

1 bulb good garlic	400 g (14 oz) fresh peas
2 teaspoons olive oil	salt and black pepper
500 g (18 oz) potatoes	1 good bunch fresh parsley, chopped
1 litre (2 pints) good vegetable stock	

Preheat the oven to 200°C/400°F/Gas Mark 6. Peel the outer dry flaky bits of skin from the garlic, keeping the bulb intact. Cut the top quarter off the bulb and discard. Place the bulb on a piece of foil and drizzle with the oil. Wrap the bulb loosely in the foil and roast in the oven for 30–45 minutes or until the cloves are soft.

Meanwhile, peel and chop the potatoes and place in a saucepan with the stock. Simmer for 20 minutes, then add the peas, seasoning and parsley, and simmer for another 10 minutes.

When the cooked garlic has cooled a little, squeeze the softened centres of the cloves out into a bowl and mix with a little of the hot stock. Add the diluted garlic to the saucepan and stir well, then remove from the heat and leave to cool slightly. Pour half of the soup into an electric blender and purée until smooth. Mix with the rest of the soup in the pan and heat through.

NOTES AND TIPS
✦ *Try this soup using chopped leeks instead of peas.*

Lentil, Squash and Carrot Soup

<u>SERVES 4</u>

CALORIES: 250	PROTEIN: HIGH
TOTAL FAT: 4.4 g	CARBOHYDRATE: ★★★
SATURATED FAT: 0.6 g	FIBRE: 7.7 g

MANY people think of lentils in the same terms as they think of, say, soya milk – as something healthy (which they certainly are) but not incredibly palatable. This is a shame, because lentils are one of the most flavoursome plant foods of all – gutsy, butch food for real men (and women, of course). This is particularly true of brown and green lentils; the red ones, I find, can be insipid in soups. Lentils are trouble-free – no need to soak or pre-boil – and they go wonderfully well with the sweeter root vegetables, such as carrots and parsnips, and with squash. This soup is about as healthy as you can get!

225 g (8 oz) (dry weight) brown or green or Puy lentils (or a mix of all three)	800 ml (28 fl oz) vegetable stock
	2 medium carrots, chopped
1 tablespoon groundnut or corn oil	200 g (7 oz) orange-fleshed squash, e.g. butternut or Turk's turban, peeled, de-seeded and cut into chunks
1 large onion, finely chopped	
1 stick celery, chopped	
1 clove garlic, chopped	salt and black pepper

Wash the lentils and drain. Heat the oil in a saucepan, add the onion, celery and garlic, and cook, stirring, for a few minutes until softened. Add the lentils and stir, then add the stock, carrots and squash, and simmer for 45 minutes or until everything is tender. Season, and leave to cool slightly. Pour two-thirds of the soup into an electric blender and purée until smooth. Mix with the rest of the soup in the saucepan and heat through. Check the seasoning and adjust, if necessary, before serving.

OPPOSITE Saffron Fish Soup (page 24), accompanied by Feta and Watercress Pâté (page 30) with Italian Bread

Crumble-Topped Aubergines

SERVES 4

CALORIES: 142	PROTEIN: MEDIUM
TOTAL FAT: 11 g	CARBOHYDRATE: ★
SATURATED FAT: 2 g	FIBRE: 1.9 g

ROBUST and flavourful if used in the right way, aubergines have too often been served heavily soaked in gallons of fat or lost in a stodgy moussaka. There are plenty of alternatives; this recipe is just one of them.

2 small aubergines	2 tablespoons pine nuts
1½ tablespoons olive oil	1 tablespoon finely chopped fresh parsley
4 tablespoons slightly stale breadcrumbs	salt and black pepper
2 tablespoons freshly grated Parmesan cheese	

Preheat the grill. Top and tail the aubergines and cut them into round 1 cm (½ inch) slices. Lay the aubergine slices on the grill and brush with some of the oil. Grill for a few minutes until golden, then turn the slices over, brush with the remaining oil and grill again.

Meanwhile, mix together the remaining ingredients. When the aubergine slices are ready, spoon the crumb mixture on top of them. Return to the grill for a few minutes or until the topping is golden. Serve immediately.

TIP
✦ *Serve on a bed of salad leaves as a dinner-party starter.*

OPPOSITE *Tabbouleh with Grilled Halloumi (page 34) served with a bowl of Tzatziki (page 119)*

Mushrooms with Herbed Couscous Stuffing

<u>SERVES 4</u>

CALORIES: 71	PROTEIN: HIGH
TOTAL FAT: 2.9 g	CARBOHYDRATE: ★★
SATURATED FAT: 0.4 g	FIBRE: 1.6 g

LIKE aubergines, mushrooms will soak up as much fat as you give them, but there is no need to cook them like that. Succulent fresh field mushrooms will bake very well.

4 large, very fresh flat mushrooms	2 spring onions, finely chopped
30 g (1¼ oz) couscous	salt and black pepper
a little boiling vegetable stock	2 teaspoons olive oil
1 tomato, de-seeded and chopped	25 g (1 oz) Fontina or half-fat mozzarella cheese
1 tablespoon finely chopped fresh parsley	

Remove the stalks from the mushrooms and chop the stalks finely. Put the couscous in a bowl and pour over enough boiling vegetable stock to cover it well. Leave to soak until the stock has been absorbed.

Preheat the oven to 190°C/375°F/Gas Mark 5. Mix the couscous with the tomato, parsley, onions, mushroom stalks and seasoning. Brush the outside of each mushroom with a little of the olive oil, and then fill each with a quarter of the couscous filling to cover the gills of the mushrooms completely. Cut the cheese into small pieces and dot over the filling. Bake in the oven for 15 minutes or until the mushrooms are tender and the cheese has melted. Serve immediately.

TIP

✦ *For a lower-calorie, lower-fat starter you could omit the cheese and bake the mushrooms wrapped in loose foil parcels so that the couscous doesn't dry out.*

Tuna Pâté

SERVES 4

CALORIES: **86**	PROTEIN: HIGH
TOTAL FAT: **2.7 g**	CARBOHYDRATE: ★
SATURATED FAT: **0.4 g**	FIBRE: **0.2 g**

TUNA is a very handy storecupboard ingredient with many uses. This quick
pâté is ideal for last-minute guests, or when you want something tangy for an
easy sandwich filling.

1 × 200 g (7 oz) can tuna in brine, drained	1 teaspoon lemon juice
50 g (2 oz) low-fat fromage frais	2 teaspoons sundried tomato paste
50 g (2 oz) virtually fat-free mayonnaise	salt and black pepper

Simply mash all the ingredients together well in a bowl, seasoning with
pepper and just a little salt if required (see Note, below). Chill before serving.

NOTES AND TIPS

✦ *Added salt may not be necessary in this recipe as there is a reasonable amount of salt
in many of the ingredients.*

✦ *The pâté would be nice served with slices of toasted Italian olive bread or with
French toast.*

Feta and Watercress Pâté

SERVES 4

CALORIES: 166	PROTEIN: HIGH
TOTAL FAT: 13 g	CARBOHYDRATE: ★
SATURATED FAT: 8.8 g	FIBRE: 0.3 g

GREEK feta is a medium-fat cheese that can be used in many dishes other than the traditional Greek salad. This pâté is very quick and easy.

1 bunch watercress	100 g (3½ oz) half-fat crème fraîche
150 g (5½ oz) feta cheese, crumbled	black pepper
25 g (1 oz) Danish Blue or Dolcelatte cheese, crumbled	

Set aside four sprigs of the watercress for the garnish. Remove the stalks from the remainder and chop the leaves. In a bowl, beat together the cheeses with the crème fraîche, then mix in the chopped watercress and season with pepper. Chill for an hour or so, then serve garnished with the sprigs of watercress.

NOTES AND TIPS
✦ *Try the same recipe using chopped black olives instead of watercress. Make sure that the olives are well rinsed, otherwise the pâté might be too salty.*
✦ *Serve with toasted pitta breads.*

Crostini with Red Peppers

SERVES 4

CALORIES: 413	PROTEIN: MEDIUM
TOTAL FAT: 15 g	CARBOHYDRATE: ★★★
SATURATED FAT: 2.4 g	FIBRE: 4.7 g

WHEN your tastebuds really need waking up, this is the starter or finger food to do it.

8 × 1 cm (½ inch) thick slices bread cut from a French or Italian country-style baguette

2 tablespoons olive oil

2 large red peppers, de-seeded and halved

50 g (2 oz) ready-made black olive tapenade (see Note, below)

1 tablespoon chopped fresh coriander

Preheat the oven to 200°C/400°F/Gas Mark 6. Brush the bread slices on both sides with most of the olive oil. Brush the remaining oil on the outsides of the red pepper halves. Place the bread and the pepper halves on a baking tray and bake in the oven. Remove the bread slices after about 10 minutes, when they are golden, and remove the pepper halves after about 25 minutes, when they are soft and the skin is beginning to bubble. Place the pepper halves in a plastic food bag. When the bread slices have cooled, spread one side of each with the olive tapenade.

When the peppers are cool enough to handle, skin and slice the pieces and arrange some on each crostini. Top with the coriander, and serve immediately while the peppers are still slightly warm.

NOTES AND TIPS

✦ *You can make your own olive tapenade if you like by puréeing stoned black olives, olive oil, garlic and one or two anchovies with a little parsley in an electric blender.*

✦ *For a short-cut, use canned or bottled peppers – slice them and stir-fry quickly in a little olive oil.*

CHAPTER THREE

SNACKS AND LUNCHES

These days few of us have time to prepare elaborate lunches, and instead rely more and more on convenience foods and takeaway sandwiches. Occasionally, however, it is nice to prepare something for yourself – perhaps at weekends when you have more time you could try some of the salad ideas in this chapter, or instead of raiding the freezer, try the quick pan pizza recipe on page 39 (or get the kids to make it!). When time really is at a premium, try my baked potato and egg ideas.

Lunch is an important meal, providing all-important energy to get you through the rest of the day, but it shouldn't be so heavy that you feel like going to sleep afterwards. If you do have to rely on a packed lunch sometimes, here are some quick ideas for livening up your meal:

+ Try a variety of different breads, not just white or wholemeal. Black rye bread is full of goodness and its firm texture and robust flavour make it ideal for open sandwiches. Pitta breads make good lunch pockets, and bagels and muffins are good too.

+ Spread your bread with something other than butter (or similar) for a change. Try sundried tomato paste and then fill with tuna and salad, or tapenade and then fill with chicken and avocado, or hummus and then fill with egg and tomato.

+ Take home-made soup to work in a wide-necked flask, or take a dip or pâté and crudités.

+ Make a quick fruit salad at home with apples, oranges, grapes and melon, pour on a little orange juice and take to work in a leakproof container.

Most of the salad recipes in this chapter are quite portable. Here are a few other salad ideas that will carry well: wild rice mixed with nuts, seeds, pulses and fruit; home-made coleslaw tossed in yogurt and lemon dressing with cashews and cold sliced potato; chopped smoked trout (hot-smoked, not the smoked salmon imitation), stirred into a mixture of horseradish and light mayonnaise, and tossed with chicory leaves and croûtons.

None but the most robust of salad leaves last well in a mixed salad for hours, so go for firmer raw vegetables such as cabbages, pak choi, chicory, radicchio, radishes, cucumber, onions, carrots and peppers.

If you're keeping an eye on your weight or the amount of fat you are eating, remember that many traditional salad dressings are high in fat, particularly full-fat mayonnaise and traditional French dressing with its high oil content. Lower-fat versions are available or you can make your own dressings based on natural low-fat bio yogurt mixed with flavourings such as lemon juice, Dijon mustard, balsamic vinegar, lime juice or tomato paste, chilli sauce or crushed garlic.

When making up your lunch, remember that to be nutritionally well balanced and to sustain you through the day, it needs to contain some protein (e.g. cheese, egg, nuts, seeds, pulses, fish), some carbohydrate (bread, rice, pasta, potato, etc.), a little fat (present in many protein foods and also supplied in your salad dressing, your bread spread, etc.) and plenty of fresh fruit and/or vegetables and/or salad.

If you want a quick hot lunch, baked potatoes can be filled with Feta and Watercress Pâté (page 30), Tuna Pâté (page 29), Tzatziki (Greek yogurt mixed with garlic and cucumber) or avocado mashed with fromage frais, all served with salad. Toast can be topped with any grilled vegetable and sprinkled with cheese, or topped with canned lentil dhal. *Ciabatta* rolls can be halved, toasted and used as quick pizza bases with your favourite topping. Any of the soups in Chapter One can be used as lunches; most will freeze. Serve with bread and fruit for a substantial midday meal.

Tabbouleh with Grilled Halloumi

SERVES 4

CALORIES: 413	PROTEIN: HIGH
TOTAL FAT: 19 g	CARBOHYDRATE: ★★
SATURATED FAT: 9 g	FIBRE: 1.6 g

I THINK it is the mint and cucumber that makes tabbouleh taste so wonderful, and the halloumi adds interesting contrast.

200 g (7 oz) bulghar wheat	2 tablespoons olive oil
3 medium tomatoes, de-seeded and chopped	2 tablespoons lemon juice
I red onion, finely chopped	salt and black pepper
8 cm (3 inch) piece cucumber, chopped	I romaine or cos lettuce, sliced
2 tablespoons chopped fresh parsley	200 g (7 oz) halloumi cheese
2 tablespoons chopped fresh mint	

Put the bulghar in a bowl and pour on enough boiling water to cover well. Leave to stand for 20 minutes, then drain well. Stir the next eight ingredients into the wheat. Arrange the lettuce in serving bowls and divide the tabbouleh between them. Heat the grill. Slice the cheese into thickish slices and grill, turning once, until golden. Chop roughly and divide between the salads. Serve at once.

Mediterranean Pasta Salad

CALORIES: 296	PROTEIN: MEDIUM
TOTAL FAT: 7.5 g	CARBOHYDRATE: ★★★
SATURATED FAT: 0.5 g	FIBRE: 2.9 g

ARTICHOKE hearts in jars are one of my main storecupboard standbys, not just because they are so more-ish but because they offer a little bit of luxury to any dish for not too huge a cost. They go particularly well with pasta and red peppers.

225 g (8 oz) fusilli, plain and spinach mixed

100 g (3½ oz) half-fat mozzarella cheese

1 × 275 g (9½ oz) jar artichoke hearts in oil, well drained (oil reserved)

1 × 275 g (9½ oz) can or jar mixed peppers, drained and roughly chopped

2 tablespoons chopped fresh basil

1 tablespoon white wine vinegar

salt and black pepper

Cook the pasta in plenty of lightly salted boiling water for 10 minutes or as directed on the packet. Meanwhile, cut the cheese into small pieces and prepare the rest of the ingredients. When the pasta is cooked, drain it and tip it into a serving bowl. Add the cheese and stir, then add the remaining ingredients with 2 tablespoons of the reserved artichoke oil. Toss well, and serve while still warm.

Smoked Mackerel Salad

SERVES 4

CALORIES: 354	PROTEIN: HIGH
TOTAL FAT: 28 g	CARBOHYDRATE: ★
SATURATED FAT: 5.6 g	FIBRE: 2.0 g

MACKEREL is an under-used food. I expect most people think of it in terms of 'all those bones' and of over-strong cooking smells, but fillets are widely available and smoked mackerel, of course, needs no cooking. It is the highest Omega-3 oily fish there is, and so well worth eating for your heart's sake.

300 g (10 oz) peppered smoked mackerel fillets	4 cm (1½ inch) piece cucumber, chopped
1 large red dessert apple	1 tablespoon lemon juice
4 sticks celery, chopped	2 teaspoons cream of horseradish sauce
25 g (1 oz) pistachio nuts	2 tablespoons natural low-fat bio yogurt
1 cos lettuce heart, chopped	salt and black pepper

Skin the mackerel fillets and break into pieces. Core the apple and cut into small bite-sized pieces, leaving the skin on. Put the fish and apple in a serving bowl with the celery, nuts, lettuce and cucumber. Beat together the remaining ingredients and combine well with the salad.

Couscous with Roast Tomatoes and Garlic

<u>SERVES 4</u>

CALORIES: 260	PROTEIN: MEDIUM
TOTAL FAT: 7.6 g	CARBOHYDRATE: ★★★
SATURATED FAT: 1.0 g	FIBRE: 2.6 g

ALTHOUGH couscous is always thought of as a Moroccan dish, the tiny grain that we call couscous is actually a pasta-like mix, so no wonder it goes so well with Italian flavours such as tomatoes, olives, basil and garlic, as in this yummy recipe.

400 g (14 oz) small tasty tomatoes (about 25 g/1 oz each)	200 g (7 oz) couscous
12 cloves good garlic, skin on	350 ml (12 fl oz) boiling vegetable stock
2 tablespoons extra-virgin olive oil	8 black olives, stoned and chopped
salt and black pepper	1 tablespoon white wine vinegar
	1 tablespoon chopped fresh basil

Preheat the oven to 200°C/400°F/Gas Mark 6. Halve the tomatoes and put them in a baking dish with the garlic cloves scattered in between. Drizzle over some of the olive oil, and season. Roast for 30 minutes or until everything is soft and tinged golden.

Meanwhile, put the couscous in a heatproof bowl, pour on the boiling stock and leave to soak. When the stock has been absorbed, stir in the remaining olive oil, the olives, wine vinegar and basil. When the tomatoes are ready, remove the garlic cloves and stir the tomatoes with any pan juices into the couscous. Squeeze the softened garlic out of the outer cases of the cloves straight into the couscous, stirring a little to combine. Serve the salad warm or at room temperature.

NOTE

✦ *From this beginning you can add all kinds of things to make a heartier meal. Roasted aubergine or courgette chunks would make tasty additions, as would roasted red onion. For some extra protein, try adding chopped hard-boiled egg or chick peas. If you eat poultry, little slices of free-range roast chicken would also be delicious in this salad.*

Fruit and Nut Rice

CALORIES: 446	PROTEIN: LOW
TOTAL FAT: 15 g	CARBOHYDRATE: ★★★
SATURATED FAT: 1.6 g	FIBRE: 4.4 g

THIS rice salad is dressed in an especially good dressing of hummus thinned down with half-fat Greek yogurt. Sounds strange, but it adds interest and delicious flavour to the salad.

225 g (8 oz) quick-cook brown rice	2 tablespoons good-quality hummus
100 g (3½ oz) beansprouts	4 tablespoons natural low-fat bio yogurt (runny,
50 g (2 oz) pecan nuts, halved	not set)
1 tablespoon sunflower seeds or pine nuts	salt and black pepper
8 no-need-to-soak dried apricot halves, chopped	2 teaspoons lemon juice
1 large banana	

Cook the brown rice in lightly salted boiling water as instructed on the packet, until tender. Drain if necessary, leave to cool a little, then spoon into a bowl and mix in the beansprouts, nuts, seeds or pine nuts and apricots. Peel and chop the banana and add to the salad. Mix the hummus with the yogurt, seasoning and lemon juice, and toss with the salad.

NOTE

✦ *Don't peel and slice or chop bananas, apples, avocado or many other fruits until ready to dress or eat, or the cut sides will oxidise (go brown) and look unattractive. This is a sign that the fruit is losing its vitamin C, so avoid cut and bruised fruit for health reasons, too.*

Pan-Cooked Pizza

<u>SERVES 4</u>

CALORIES: 336	PROTEIN: MEDIUM
TOTAL FAT: 12 g	CARBOHYDRATE: ★★★
SATURATED FAT: 1.7 g	FIBRE: 2.6 g

To make this pizza, you will need a suitable non-stick frying pan with a heatproof handle as the top of the pizza has to be finished off under the grill.

225 g (8 oz) self-raising flour

salt

100 g (3½ oz) grated half-fat mozzarella cheese

3 tablespoons light olive oil

half quantity Home-Made Tomato Sauce with
  Mushrooms (see page 107) or about 200 g (7 oz)
  bottled Italian tomato and mushroom pizza sauce

4 stoned black olives, sliced

2 tomatoes, sliced

2 teaspoons chopped fresh basil or oregano

Sift the flour with some salt into a mixing bowl and add a quarter of the grated cheese, 1 tablespoon of the oil and 5 tablespoons water. Mix together with a fork, adding a very little more water if necessary to form a dough. Roll the dough out on a floured surface to form a round the right size to fit the base of your non-stick frying pan.

Heat 1 tablespoon of the remaining oil in the frying pan and, when hot, add the dough base and cook over a medium heat for a few minutes until the underneath is golden. Remove the dough, add the remaining oil to the pan and, when hot, fry the other side of the dough until golden. Heat the grill. Spread the tomato sauce on the dough in the pan, and top with the olives, sliced tomatoes and herbs. Finish with the remaining cheese, then flash under the grill for a few minutes until the cheese is bubbling. Serve immediately.

NOTES AND TIPS
◆ *Serve with salad.*
◆ *You could add some sliced fresh mushrooms to the pizza, or some sliced artichoke hearts or drained canned peppers.*

Mr Herbert's Baked Potatoes

SERVES 4

CALORIES: 328	PROTEIN: MEDIUM
TOTAL FAT: 13 g	CARBOHYDRATE: ★★★
SATURATED FAT: 2.7 g	FIBRE: 7.6 g (INCLUDING POTATO SKIN)

MR Herbert is my son's guitar tutor. He is a vegetarian and I asked him for a scrumptious recipe to include in this book. This is it. Well, actually his original recipe included lots of butter, too, but in the interests of everyone watching their saturated fat intake, I decided it wasn't strictly necessary.

4 medium baking potatoes	4 tablespoons thick natural bio yogurt
4 tablespoons organic crunchy peanut butter	I pack fresh alfalfa sprouts

Preheat the oven to 200°C/400°F/Gas Mark 6. Prick the potatoes and bake them in the oven for 1–1½ hours or until the skins are nice and crisp and the centres perfectly soft. When the potatoes are ready, warm the peanut butter very slightly in a small pan and beat in the yogurt. Cut a large cross in each potato and fill with the peanut mixture. Top with as many sprouts as you like and serve immediately.

NOTE

✦ *You could, of course, cook the potatoes in the microwave to save time, but when cooking four potatoes I find that in fact you don't save all that many minutes, and the results lack the crispy finish of traditionally baked potatoes.*

Twice-Baked Potatoes

SERVES 4

CALORIES: 424	PROTEIN: HIGH
TOTAL FAT: 17 g	CARBOHYDRATE: ★★
SATURATED FAT: 5.6 g	FIBRE: 6.8 g (INCLUDING POTATO SKIN)

TRY these for a special weekend lunch treat if you have children. Everybody loves them!

4 medium baking potatoes	200 g (7 oz) reduced-fat Cheddar cheese, grated
2 tablespoons corn oil	2 teaspoons Dijon mustard
1 medium onion, finely chopped	2 tablespoons natural low-fat bio yogurt
4 tablespoons vegetarian herb sausage mix	salt and black pepper
100 g (3½ oz) mushrooms, chopped	

Preheat the oven to 200°C/400°F/Gas Mark 6. Prick the potatoes and bake them in the oven for 1–1½ hours or until the skins are nice and crisp and the centres soft. About 15 minutes before the end of the cooking time, heat the oil in a non-stick frying pan and sauté the onion for 5 minutes or until soft and just turning golden. Add the sausage mix and mushrooms, and sauté again until the 'sausage' is lightly browned.

When the potatoes are cooked, take them out of the oven and halve lengthways. Scoop out most of the flesh (reserve the skins), and mix in a bowl with the onion mixture, half the cheese, the mustard, yogurt and seasoning to taste. Pile the mixture back into the skins and top with the rest of the cheese. Place the potato halves on a baking tray and return to the oven for 10 minutes or until the cheese is bubbling and golden. Serve straight away.

NOTES AND TIPS
+ *Serve with a green or tomato salad.*
+ *You could make up your own combination of ingredients to mix with the potato flesh. You could also try using the same recipe with orange-fleshed sweet potatoes, which are totally delicious and full of beta-carotene (but their skins don't crisp up like ordinary potatoes).*

Spanish Omelette

<u>SERVES 4</u>

CALORIES: 304	PROTEIN: HIGH
TOTAL FAT: 17 g	CARBOHYDRATE: ★
SATURATED FAT: 3.4 g	FIBRE: 2.2 g

I SUPPOSE Spanish omelette could be seen as a continental version of egg and chips, so no wonder children love it. Eggs are medium-high in fat but full of good nutrients, so it is worth incorporating them in our diets now and then. You will need a large non-stick frying pan with a heatproof handle as this omelette has to be finished off under the grill.

500 g (18 oz) potatoes, peeled	salt and black pepper
2 tablespoons corn oil or light olive oil	8 medium free-range eggs
1 onion, thinly sliced	1 clove garlic, crushed (optional)

Cut the potatoes into chunks and boil them in salted water for about 15 minutes or until just tender. Drain the potatoes and slice them roughly into 0.5 cm (¼ inch) rounds. Heat half the oil in a large non-stick frying pan and sauté the onion for about 5 minutes or until it is soft and just turning golden. Push the onion to one side, add the potato slices and sauté for about 10 minutes or until they too are tinged with gold. Mix the onions and potatoes in the pan, season and add the rest of the oil. While the oil heats, switch on the grill to preheat and beat the eggs with a very little cold water and seasoning (and garlic if using). Pour the eggs evenly over the potatoes and onions, and cook over a medium heat for a few minutes until the egg sets and the base is brown. Flash the omelette under the grill for a minute or two until the top is cooked and golden. Don't overcook or it will be unpalatably dry. Serve in wedges.

NOTES AND TIPS
- ✦ *Serve with crusty bread, if liked, and salad.*
- ✦ *Some people add other things, such as red peppers, to their Spanish omelette, but the traditional version is just potatoes, onion and eggs.*

Unusual Scrambled Eggs

SERVES 4

CALORIES: **327**	PROTEIN: HIGH
TOTAL FAT: **20 g**	CARBOHYDRATE: ★
SATURATED FAT: **7 g**	FIBRE: 1.9 g

The person who gave me this recipe – yes, it was Mr Herbert (see page 40) – eats this version of scrambled eggs for breakfast, claiming the garlic in it sets him up well for the day ahead! You may prefer to be more conservative and have it for lunch or supper. Either way, I have to admit these eggs are surprisingly good.

20 g (¾ oz) butter	2 cloves garlic, well crushed
8 large free-range eggs	4 slices wholemeal bread
4 tablespoons bio yogurt or Greek yogurt	

Melt half the butter in a non-stick saucepan. Beat the eggs with the yogurt and garlic, add to the pan and cook over a medium-low heat, stirring occasionally. Meanwhile, toast the bread and spread with the remaining butter. When the egg is scrambled but still nice and moist, pile it on to the slices of toast and serve immediately.

CHAPTER FOUR

FISH AND SEAFOOD

Fish has always been perceived as a 'healthy' food, and so it is, but it has never achieved the popularity of other 'health' foods, perhaps because people think it is boring. In fact, in fish's favour, I must say straight away that a fresh fish cooked simply, with perhaps nothing more than lemon juice and seasoning, is usually far from boring.

When choosing fish, try to make sure you get the best-quality, freshest fish you can so you can be sure it will have the best flavour and texture possible. Find a fishmonger or supermarket counter you feel you can trust, and be prepared to change your mind about what you are going to cook if the fishmonger has something better on offer. Never buy fish that smells 'fishy' – it is probably far from fresh. The quality of some frozen fish is okay but, once it has been frozen, it is very hard to tell whether a piece of fish is good or not.

Amongst the many benefits of fish are that it is high in protein, and either low in fat or high in beneficial Omega-3 oil. It is also quick to cook, and, although fish is no longer a cheap option, fish farming has brought down the price of some fish such as salmon and trout. But the absolute *best* thing about fish is the amazing variety of types now available. I tried pike for the first time the other day, and found it marvellously flavoursome and dense – a real find *and* inexpensive too. So give fish the chance it deserves; the recipes in this chapter are just an example of how flexible it can be.

If you haven't got time for a recipe, however, here are a few ideas for quick and simple but delicious ways to cook fish: simply grill fish with a little olive oil and chopped herbs, e.g. sardines with parsley, cod with coriander or salmon with basil; dry-fry oily fish in a pan with seasoning, and serve with a quick sauce such as mashed avocado and Greek yogurt or a tomato salsa; bake fillets of brill, mullet or monkfish in foil with chopped onion, parsley, lemon juice, seasoning and olive oil.

Not all the fish and seafood recipes in this book are in this chapter; you will find other recipes featuring fish in the chapter on soups and starters, snacks and lunches, pasta, and rice and grains.

Shellfish is one of the quickest foods imaginable and, like white fish, extremely low in fat. Scallops take just seconds to flash fry or grill; prawns a minute or two longer. Try them on kebab sticks with a baste of chilli oil – delicious!

Swordfish, Potato and Olive Gratin

CALORIES: **386**	PROTEIN: HIGH
TOTAL FAT: **15 g**	CARBOHYDRATE: ★
SATURATED FAT: **2.7 g**	FIBRE: **3.1 g**

SWORDFISH is my favourite firm white fish, but you could easily use cod, halibut, monkfish or shark in this recipe.

600 g (22 oz) potatoes, peeled	4 swordfish steaks (about 700 g/1½ lb total weight)
2 tablespoons light olive oil	24 stoned black olives, well rinsed
1 onion, thinly sliced	juice of ½ lemon
2 cloves garlic, crushed	salt and black pepper

Preheat the oven to 190°C/375°F/Gas Mark 5. Boil the potatoes in lightly salted water for 15–20 minutes or until barely tender. Drain, cool slightly, then slice into thickish rounds. Heat most of the oil in a non-stick frying pan and sauté the onion for 5–10 minutes or until soft and just turning golden. Add the garlic and stir for 1 minute. Brush a suitably sized gratin dish with the remaining oil and arrange the potatoes over the base. Put the fish on top and scatter the onion and olives around. Squeeze the lemon juice over and season well. Bake in the oven for 20 minutes or until the fish is cooked through.

Tangy Cod Fillets

SERVES 4

CALORIES: 188	PROTEIN: HIGH
TOTAL FAT: 4.1 g	CARBOHYDRATE: ★
SATURATED FAT: 0.6 g	FIBRE: 0.7 g

YOU will find an unusual ingredient – marmalade – in this dish. Don't be put off by it – it gives the cod a noticeable, but not overpowering, tang.

I tablespoon corn oil	I tablespoon lemon juice
I medium leek, thinly sliced into rounds	I tablespoon orange marmalade
I clove garlic, chopped	salt and black pepper
4 × 175 g (6 oz) cod fillets	

Heat the oil in a non-stick frying pan and sauté the leek and garlic for a few minutes until softened. Move the leeks to one side, add the fish fillets, skin sides up, and cook without moving for a few minutes or until they are tinged golden. Turn over and continue cooking for another few minutes until the fish is opaque all the way through (the time needed depending upon the thickness of your fillets). When cooked, remove the fillets from the pan and place on serving plates. Add the lemon juice, marmalade and seasoning to the pan and stir for a minute, then tip the citrus/leek sauce around the fish. Serve immediately.

NOTE
✦ *Fish other than cod can be used – coley, haddock or monkfish would all be fine.*

Smoky Fishburgers

SERVES 4

CALORIES: **286**	PROTEIN: HIGH
TOTAL FAT: **4.5 g**	CARBOHYDRATE: ★★
SATURATED FAT: **1.6 g**	FIBRE: **1.5 g**

EVERYONE loves fishcakes. Here's a variation using both smoked and white fish to make an ideal midweek family supper.

225 g (8 oz) smoked haddock fillet	I tablespoon chopped fresh parsley or chives
225 g (8 oz) coley or cod fillet	I medium egg, beaten
225 g (8 oz) mashed potatoes (made using semi-skimmed milk)	2 teaspoons plain flour
	40 g (1½ oz) half-fat Cheddar cheese, grated
2 spring onions, finely chopped	100 g (3½ oz) slightly stale breadcrumbs

Remove any pieces of skin from the fish and cut into small pieces. In a bowl, mix together both types of fish, the potatoes, spring onions, parsley or chives and egg. Divide the mixture into eight and, using hands dusted with the flour, shape into patties. Mix together the cheese and breadcrumbs and put on a flat plate. Coat each burger in the crumb mixture, then arrange on a baking tray and place in the freezer for about 1 hour or until really cold.

Preheat the oven to 190°C/375°F/Gas Mark 5. Bake the fishburgers in the oven for 20 minutes or until cooked through and the coating is golden.

NOTES AND TIPS

✦ *You can make tasty burgers this way using salmon fillet instead of smoked fish, which will increase the fat and calorie content a little but will provide more Omega-3 fats than the above recipe.*

✦ *Serve with home-made oven chips and peas, or just a selection of vegetables.*

Fricasée of Three Fish

SERVES 4

CALORIES: 293	PROTEIN: HIGH
TOTAL FAT: 10 g	CARBOHYDRATE: ★
SATURATED FAT: 3.1 g	FIBRE: 1.1 g

450 g (1 lb) new potatoes

200 g (7 oz) salmon fillet, skinned

200 g (7 oz) coley or cod fillet, skinned

100 ml (3½ fl oz) fish stock

pinch of saffron strands

200 g (7 oz) frozen mixed green beans, peas, carrots and sweetcorn

100 g (3½ oz) cooked peeled prawns

1 tablespoon chopped fresh dill or tarragon

2 tablespoons half-fat crème fraîche

salt and black pepper

Cut the potatoes into bite-sized chunks, if necessary, and cook them in lightly salted boiling water for about 20 minutes or until tender. Drain well.

Cut the fish into bite-sized chunks and place in a pan with the fish stock and saffron strands. Bring to a simmer and simmer gently for a few minutes. Meanwhile, cook the mixed vegetables until just tender in lightly salted boiling water, adding the prawns for the last minute to heat through. Drain and mix with the potatoes. When the salmon and white fish are cooked, remove from the pan and combine with the vegetables and prawns. Arrange on serving plates. Stir the herbs, crème fraîche and seasoning into the stock remaining in the pan, and heat through. Check the seasoning and pour a quarter of the sauce over each serving of fish and vegetables.

Creamy Fish Curry

SERVES 4

CALORIES: 263	PROTEIN: HIGH
TOTAL FAT: 11 g	CARBOHYDRATE: ★
SATURATED FAT: 2.5 g	FIBRE: 1 g

THIS curry is based on the typical Thai flavours of chilli, lime, coriander and ginger, but manages to be much lower in fat than authentic Thai curries which are almost always laden with coconut milk. I've simply used half-fat Greek yogurt instead to produce that creamy texture, and it works very well.

2 tablespoons groundnut oil	2 teaspoons Thai fish sauce
1 medium onion, finely chopped	800 g (1¾ lb) firm white fish, e.g. monkfish or
2 cloves garlic, crushed	swordfish, cut into bite-sized cubes
2 tablespoons Thai red curry paste (see Note,	200 ml (7 fl oz) fish stock
below)	juice of 1 lime
1 good red chilli, de-seeded and chopped	4 tablespoons half-fat Greek yogurt
1 rounded teaspoon grated fresh ginger	2 tablespoons chopped fresh coriander
2 medium tomatoes, de-seeded and chopped	salt (optional)

Heat the oil in a large non-stick frying pan and sauté the onion for 5 minutes or until soft and just turning golden. Add the garlic, curry paste, chilli and ginger and cook, stirring, for 2 minutes, then add the tomatoes, fish sauce and fish, and stir for 1 minute. Pour in the stock and lime juice, bring to a simmer and cook for a few minutes until the fish is tender. Stir in the yogurt and coriander and check the seasoning, adding a little salt if required.

NOTES AND TIPS

✦ *You could make your own Thai red curry paste if you like but I find that if you buy a good-quality ready-made paste and combine it in the recipe with the garlic, chilli, etc., it is just as good. You could also try adding chopped fresh lemon grass with the curry paste.*

✦ *Serve with Thai fragrant rice and a cucumber salad.*

Grilled Salmon with a Lentil Salsa

SERVES 4

CALORIES: 418	PROTEIN: HIGH
TOTAL FAT: 22 g	CARBOHYDRATE: ★
SATURATED FAT: 3.8 g	FIBRE: 3.4 g

BROWN lentils go particularly well with salmon. Add a few spicy flavours and you have something really special.

4 × 150 g (5 oz) salmon fillets	1 tablespoon chopped fresh coriander
2 tablespoons teriyaki marinade	1 small green chilli, de-seeded and finely chopped
100 g (3½ oz) brown lentils (see Note, below)	1 tablespoon olive oil
300 ml (½ pint) salt-free vegetable stock	juice of 1 lime
2 medium tomatoes, de-seeded and chopped	salt and black pepper
1 small red onion, finely chopped	2 teaspoons groundnut oil
4 cm (1½ inch) piece cucumber, chopped	
1 small yellow or red pepper, de-seeded and chopped	

Place the salmon fillets in a shallow dish and evenly spoon over the teriyaki marinade. Cover and leave in the fridge for 30 minutes–1 hour. Meanwhile, make the lentil salsa. Boil the lentils in the stock for 45 minutes or until tender, then drain. Stir in the remaining ingredients, except the groundnut oil, and put in a serving dish. Heat the grill to high with a baking tray underneath. Remove the salmon fillets from the marinade, place on the hot baking tray and brush the tops with the groundnut oil. Grill for 5–8 minutes (depending upon the thickness of the fish and its distance from the heat) and serve with the lentil salsa.

TIP
✦ Puy lentils are the most flavoursome lentils so use them if you can get them.

Chinese-Style Steamed Tilapia

<u>SERVES 4</u>

CALORIES: 169	PROTEIN: HIGH
TOTAL FAT: 5.1 g	CARBOHYDRATE: ★
SATURATED FAT: 0.9 g	FIBRE: 0.3 g

I THINK tilapia are the best single-serving whole fish you can get – low on awkward bones, high on tasty flesh and not too expensive. They don't need a lot of flavours added, but as they come from oriental waters, these Chinese-style flavours complement them brilliantly.

4 medium tilapia, prepared for cooking	1 tablespoon soy sauce
4 large spring onions, finely chopped	1 tablespoon rice wine or dry sherry
4 cm (1½ inch) piece fresh ginger, peeled and grated	1 tablespoon sesame oil
	salt and black pepper
1 mild red chilli, de-seeded and chopped	1 teaspoon cornflour

Put the fish on heatproof plates that will fit inside your steamer (see Note, below). Place half the spring onions, ginger and chilli inside the fish, then sprinkle the rest on top. Sprinkle the soy sauce, rice wine or sherry and sesame oil over the fish and season well. Cover and steam for 8–10 minutes or until the fish is cooked. Pour the fish juices that have collected on the plates into a small saucepan. Blend the cornflour to a paste with a little cold water, add it to the fish juices and heat through, stirring, until a thin sauce has formed. Pour the sauce over the fish and serve immediately.

NOTES AND TIPS
✦ *If you don't have suitable steaming equipment, you can follow the same recipe but put the fish in individual foil parcels instead of on plates, and bake in the oven at 180°C/350°F/Gas Mark 4 for 15 minutes or until cooked. Collect the juices from inside the foil and proceed as above.*
✦ *Serve with some rice or noodles and broccoli.*

Traditional Fish Pie

SERVES 4

CALORIES: 369	PROTEIN: HIGH
TOTAL FAT: 10 g	CARBOHYDRATE: ★
SATURATED FAT: 5 g	FIBRE: 2.2 g

THIS is one of my all-time favourite dishes, and I'm sure I'm not alone. There is nothing to beat a creamy, cheesy white sauce with succulent fish and a crisped potato topping. This version cuts fat so it isn't a guilt-laden feast, either!

500 g (18 oz) floury potatoes	1 rounded tablespoon plain flour
50 ml (2 fl oz) semi-skimmed milk	75 g (3 oz) half-fat mature Cheddar cheese, grated
salt and black pepper	50 g (2 oz) cooked peeled prawns
450 g (1 lb) white fish fillet, cubed	2 medium eggs, hard-boiled and quartered
300 ml (½ pint) skimmed milk	100 g (3½ oz) mushrooms, sliced
200 ml (7 fl oz) fish stock or water	1 tablespoon chopped fresh parsley or dill
15 g (½ oz) butter	

Preheat the oven to 200°C/400°F/Gas Mark 6. Peel the potatoes, dice them and boil in lightly salted water for 10 minutes or until tender, then drain. Mash the potatoes with the semi-skimmed milk and seasoning, and set aside. Put the fish in a non-stick pan with the skimmed milk and fish stock or water, and simmer for 10 minutes. Remove the fish with a slotted spatula and arrange over the base of a suitably sized gratin dish.

Pour the poaching liquid through a sieve into a jug. Melt the butter in a saucepan, add the flour and stir for 1–2 minutes over a medium heat. Remove from the heat and gradually add the poaching liquid, stirring as you go, until you have a smooth sauce. Season, add two-thirds of the cheese, and stir. Check the seasoning.

Scatter the prawns, eggs, mushrooms and parsley or dill evenly over the fish and pour the cheese sauce on top, coating everything. Spoon the mashed potato around the edges of the dish, then run a fork around the surface. Sprinkle the remaining cheese over the centre of the pie and bake in the oven for about 20 minutes or until the potato and cheese are golden.

NOTES AND TIPS
✦ *If the potato starts to go too brown before the cheese is golden, cover the pie with foil.*

Provençal Tuna Steaks au Gratin

<u>SERVES 4</u>

CALORIES: 428	PROTEIN: HIGH
TOTAL FAT: 20 g	CARBOHYDRATE: ★
SATURATED FAT: 3.5 g	FIBRE: 4.8 g

THE lovely tomato flavours of the Mediterranean go very well with all white fish, and with tuna. Try to buy your tuna fresh as its texture will be much better than a frozen piece.

3 tablespoons light olive oil	600 g (22 oz) tuna steaks, cut into good-sized
I medium onion, finely chopped	chunks
2 cloves garlic, finely chopped	½ *ciabatta* or French country loaf (about
I large red pepper, de-seeded and sliced	200 g/7 oz)
I × 400 g (14 oz) can chopped tomatoes	8 stoned black olives, halved
I bulb fennel, sliced into eighths	handful of fresh basil or oregano leaves *or*
I tablespoon sundried tomato paste	I teaspoon dried oregano
200 ml (7 fl oz) fish stock	salt and black pepper

Preheat the oven to 190°C/375°F/Gas Mark 5. Heat 1 tablespoon of the oil in a large non-stick frying pan and sauté the onion with half the garlic and all the red pepper for 5–10 minutes or until soft and just turning golden. Add the chopped tomatoes, fennel, tomato paste and fish stock, and simmer for 10 minutes. Meanwhile, place the pieces of tuna in a suitable ovenproof dish. Break the bread into small pieces and combine in a bowl with the rest of the garlic and olive oil.

When the fennel is just tender, and the sauce has reduced to a fairly thick consistency, add the olives and herbs to the tomato mixture with some black pepper. Taste and add a little salt if necessary, then pour the sauce over the tuna. Scatter the bread/oil mixture evenly over the top and bake in the oven for 20 minutes or until golden.

NOTES AND TIPS

✦ *Serve with a green salad and perhaps some potatoes if you are very hungry.*

✦ *You could use aubergine or courgette instead of fennel for a change, and you could try any firm white fish instead of tuna, which would lower the calorie and fat content a little, but would also reduce the Omega-3 fat content of the recipe.*

Garlic and Chilli Prawns with Avocado Rice

SERVES 4

CALORIES: 471		PROTEIN: HIGH	
TOTAL FAT: 16 g		CARBOHYDRATE: ★	
SATURATED FAT: 3.3 g		FIBRE: 2.1 g	

ALL members of the prawn family go marvellously well with avocado; in fact all four major ingredients in this recipe were, I think, made for each other. Any good prawns will do, but small watery frozen ones won't work at all.

5 teaspoons groundnut oil	600 g (22 oz) prawns, tails on (uncooked if
juice of 2 limes	possible)
4 cloves garlic, chopped	200 g (7 oz) basmati rice
2 red chillies, de-seeded and finely chopped	1 large or 2 small avocados
black pepper	

In a shallow bowl, mix together 3 teaspoons of the oil, the juice of 1 lime, the garlic, chilli and black pepper. Toss the prawns in this marinade and leave, covered, for up to 30 minutes for the flavours to mingle.

Meanwhile, simmer the rice in 500 ml (18 fl oz) lightly salted water with the lid on the pan, checking once or twice that you don't need to add a little more boiling water, until the rice is tender and fluffy and all the water absorbed. When the rice is nearly cooked, halve, stone and peel the avocado, and chop the flesh into fairly small pieces. Toss in the remaining lime juice. Tip the rice out into a warm serving bowl (or bowls) and gently stir the avocado into the rice. Keep warm.

Remove the prawns from the marinade, reserving the marinade. Heat the remaining oil in a non-stick wok or frying pan, add the prawns, and cook over a high heat for about 3 minutes, stirring constantly until they are almost cooked. Tip the marinade into the pan, turn the heat down to medium high, and cook for a further 2 minutes, stirring all the time so the garlic doesn't burn. Serve the prawns on the avocado rice.

NOTE

✦ *If you use pre-cooked prawns, omit the 3 minutes' stir-frying.*

Stir-Fried Squid and Vegetables

SERVES 4

CALORIES: 208	PROTEIN: HIGH
TOTAL FAT: 7.9 g	CARBOHYDRATE: ★
SATURATED FAT: 1.5 g	FIBRE: 2 g

SQUID is becoming more popular and more widely available. The tubes will become tough if overcooked but with a light touch they are delicious. Squid is also extremely low in calories and fat.

125 g (4½ oz) broccoli, cut into small florets	1 rounded teaspoon Chinese five-spice seasoning
600 g (22 oz) squid tubes, cut into bite-sized pieces	1 teaspoon Tabasco pepper sauce
1 tablespoon groundnut oil	1 tablespoon light soy sauce
100 g (3½ oz) mangetout	2 teaspoons caster sugar
4 large spring onions, halved	2 teaspoons sherry vinegar
1 clove garlic, crushed	100 g (3½ oz) fresh beansprouts
2 teaspoons sesame oil	

Blanch the broccoli and squid in a little boiling water for 1 minute, then drain. Heat the groundnut oil in a non-stick wok and stir-fry the broccoli and mangetout for a few minutes until just tender. Add the spring onions, garlic, sesame oil and five-spice seasoning, and stir for a minute or two more, then add the Tabasco, soy sauce, sugar, vinegar and beansprouts. Stir again. Toss the squid into the pan and stir-fry for 30 seconds until everything is well coated in the sauce.

Shellfish Paella

SERVES 4

CALORIES: 504	PROTEIN: HIGH
TOTAL FAT: 8 g	CARBOHYDRATE: ★★★
SATURATED FAT: 1.1 g	FIBRE: 5 g

To make enough paella for four people you do need a very large frying pan or, even better, a proper paella pan with handles on both sides.

2 tablespoons olive oil	100 g (3½ oz) sliced green beans
1 Spanish onion, chopped	100 g (3½ oz) petits pois
1 yellow pepper, de-seeded and chopped	200 g (7 oz) can chopped tomatoes
1 red pepper, de-seeded and chopped	300 g (10 oz) good-quality prawns, tails on
350 g (12 oz) risotto or basmati rice	salt and black pepper
about 850 ml (29 fl oz) vegetable or fish stock	20 ready-cleaned mussels, shells on (see page 59)
1 sachet saffron strands	

Heat the oil in a large non-stick frying pan or paella pan and sauté the onion and peppers over a medium heat for 10 minutes until soft and just turning golden. Add the rice and stir to coat well with oil. Add the stock, saffron and beans, bring to a simmer, and cook gently for 20 minutes, stirring from time to time, until the rice is nearly cooked. Add the peas, tomatoes, prawns and seasoning, stir and cook for a further few minutes, adding a little extra stock if the paella dries out too much. Meanwhile, steam the mussels in a small amount of water in a covered saucepan for a few minutes or until they open. Discard any that do not open. Serve the paella topped with the mussels.

NOTES AND TIPS

✦ *You need to watch the paella carefully while it cooks as the rice can stick quite easily or dry out if you don't get the amount of liquid right.*

✦ *You can add slices of squid to the paella if you like, or use asparagus tips instead of the green beans.*

✦ *If you use risotto rice, the paella will be creamier; with basmati rice it will be more like a pilau, the grains more separate. I prefer the basmati version!*

Prawn Kebabs with Sweet–Sour Sauce

<u>SERVES 4</u>

CALORIES: 205	PROTEIN: HIGH
TOTAL FAT: 1.4 g	CARBOHYDRATE: ★
SATURATED FAT: 0.2 g	FIBRE: 1.6 g

AN easy but impressive supper dish to serve when you're short of time.

24 extra-large raw king or tiger prawns, tails on	4 tablespoons pineapple juice
12 button mushrooms	2 tablespoons light soy sauce
1 yellow pepper, de-seeded and cut into small squares	dash of Worcestershire sauce
	2 tablespoons tomato purée
1 courgette, cut into bite-sized chunks	1 tablespoon red wine vinegar
2 rounded tablespoons runny honey	1 teaspoon cornflour

Thread the prawns and vegetables alternately on to four large or eight small kebab sticks. Place in a shallow dish or bowl. Mix all the remaining ingredients, except the cornflour, together thoroughly and pour over the kebabs. Cover and leave to marinate for 30 minutes.

When ready to cook, preheat the grill to medium. Remove the kebabs from the marinade and grill for 8 minutes, turning once. Meanwhile, put the marinade in a small saucepan. Blend the cornflour with a little cold water and stir into the marinade. Heat to simmering point, stirring, until you have a rich sauce. Serve the kebabs with the sauce.

NOTES AND TIPS
✦ *These kebabs are best served with plain basmati or pilau rice and a green salad.*
✦ *This recipe doesn't really work unless the prawns are raw.*

OPPOSITE *Smoky Fishburgers (page 48) served with a herb garnish and Home-Made Tomato Sauce (page 107)*

Mussels au Gratin

SERVES 4

CALORIES: 149	PROTEIN: HIGH
TOTAL FAT: 9.6 g	CARBOHYDRATE: ★
SATURATED FAT: 1.5 g	FIBRE: 0.2 g

LIKE squid, mussels are becoming more widely available, especially the ready-cleaned kind. They are also fairly inexpensive, very low in fat, and look terrific on the plate. Here's another quick, easy recipe for you to try.

40 ready-cleaned mussels, shells on	3 tablespoons slightly stale breadcrumbs
2 cloves garlic, finely chopped	3 tablespoons light olive oil
grated rind of ½ good lemon	salt and black pepper
1 tablespoon finely chopped fresh parsley	

Bring a little water to the boil in a large saucepan. Add the mussels, cover tightly and steam for a few minutes until the shells open. Drain, and discard any mussels that have failed to open. Remove the top shell halves and arrange the mussels in a large shallow heatproof dish.

Preheat the grill to medium. In a bowl, mix together the garlic, lemon rind, parsley, breadcrumbs, oil and a little seasoning. Put a spoonful of this mixture on each mussel and smooth down to cover. Grill the mussels for a few minutes until the topping is golden. Serve immediately.

NOTES AND TIPS
+ *Make sure the crumbs are quite stale otherwise the topping won't turn golden quickly enough and the mussels will be overcooked and tough.*
+ *Serve with some lemon juice and salad for a light meal.*

OPPOSITE Garlic and Chilli Prawns with Avocado Rice (page 55)

CHAPTER FIVE

PASTA

When I was thinking about pasta before beginning to write this chapter, I realised that it probably has more attributes than almost any other food. As well as being incredibly versatile because it combines well with so many flavours, there is such a variety of different shapes, colours and sizes of pasta available that it never becomes boring. Being a low-fat, complex carbohydrate food that also contains valuable protein, vitamins and minerals, pasta is generally a healthy option that everyone, including children, enjoys. It is inexpensive, quick to cook and hard to ruin; at the end of a tiring day, a satisfying, comforting bowl of hot pasta is just what you need.

What more, really, could you ask of a food? If you haven't been making enough use of pasta in your diet, I hope this chapter will give you plenty of ideas. Most of the recipes are quick to cook but I've also included a couple that take a little longer. There are literally hundreds of different pastas and my suggestions for which type to use with each dish can be altered according to what you have or what you can buy. However, try to use heavier, thicker pastas with the chunkier sauces; delicate, thin pastas go best with the lighter, less bulky sauces.

My storecupboard always contains the following types of dried pasta: spaghetti, tagliatelle, penne, conchiglie, macaroni and papardelle, including a couple of spinach pastas and a couple of wholewheat ones which contain more fibre and B vitamins. You may also like to buy some red (tomato) pasta and some black pasta, which gets its colour from squid ink. So that you are never short of an instant meal, make sure your larder also contains a good selection of the following to make up easy pasta sauces: passata, sundried tomato paste, black and green olives, dried mushrooms, anchovies, sardines, tuna, canned peppers and artichoke hearts, capers, pine nuts, chilli sauce and, of course, olive oil and garlic or garlic purée. In the fridge, keep fresh chillies, yogurt and Parmesan or Pecorino.

Using these ingredients, here are a few very quick ideas for sauces to serve over pasta: sundried tomato paste mixed with passata, black olives and garlic purée and heated through; canned sardines, chopped and heated through with olive oil and pine nuts; ready-made tomato sauce enlivened with re-constituted *porcini* (dried mushrooms) and plenty of grated cheese; puréed canned red peppers flavoured with chilli sauce.

If you can also keep in your freezer a good selection of vegetables, such as leaf spinach, broccoli and small peas, you will be able to produce even more great pasta meals at a moment's notice. A stock of frozen Home-Made Tomato Sauce (see page 107) is also a good idea. The only things to avoid if you want your pasta to be healthy are rich creams and too much high-fat cheeses in your sauces. You needn't ban dairy produce from your pasta cooking, but it's easy to cut right down on it because there are so many other healthy flavours that enhance pasta even better.

Pasta with Fresh Tomato Sauce and Garlic Croûtons

<u>SERVES 4</u>

CALORIES: 406	PROTEIN: MEDIUM
TOTAL FAT: 11 g	CARBOHYDRATE: ★★★
SATURATED FAT: 2.5 g	FIBRE: 4.6 g

A SIMPLE and fresh-tasting sauce that really does need excellent, ripe, non-hothouse tomatoes (preferably from your own garden!) to do it justice. The skins are left on, too, so you really don't want tomatoes with tough, tasteless skins in this recipe.

600 g (22 oz) good tomatoes, halved, de-seeded
  and chopped

1 medium mild onion, finely chopped

1 clove garlic, well crushed

1 tablespoon olive oil

2 teaspoons red wine vinegar

1 teaspoon balsamic vinegar

2 tablespoons chopped fresh basil

salt and black pepper

300 g (10 oz) spaghetti or spaghettini (dry weight)

2 tablespoons freshly grated Parmesan cheese

Garlic Croûtons

4 slices good white bread, e.g. *ciabatta*

1½ tablespoons olive oil

1 large clove garlic, peeled

Preheat the oven to 180°C/350°F/Gas Mark 4. In a bowl, combine the first eight ingredients and set aside. For the croûtons, brush the bread with the olive oil and rub the garlic over the slices. Cut into squares and bake in the oven for about 10 minutes or until crisp. Meanwhile, cook the pasta in plenty of boiling salted water for 10–12 minutes or until just tender, drain and tip into a serving bowl. Spoon the tomato dressing over, toss to combine, and serve sprinkled with the cheese and croûtons.

NOTE
✦ *A simple green salad goes well with this.*

Pasta with Storecupboard Sauce

SERVES 4

CALORIES: **400**	PROTEIN: MEDIUM
TOTAL FAT: **15 g**	CARBOHYDRATE: ★★★
SATURATED FAT: **1.3 g**	FIBRE: **4 g**

WHEN the cupboard really is nearly bare because you forgot to go shopping again, try this recipe.

300 g (10 oz) penne or papardelle (dry weight)

2 rounded tablespoons sundried tomato paste

2 cloves garlic, well crushed *or* I rounded teaspoon minced garlic

½ teaspoon ground chillies *or* I teaspoon chilli sauce

50 g (2 oz) stoned green olives, well rinsed and finely chopped

black pepper

I tablespoon olive oil

½ × 400 g (14 oz) can chopped tomatoes

a few extra green olives to garnish

Cook the pasta in plenty of boiling salted water for about 12 minutes or until just tender. Meanwhile, using a pestle and mortar or an electric blender, blend together the tomato paste and garlic until well combined. Add the chillies or chilli sauce, olives and black pepper, and blend again, then mix in the olive oil and finally mix everything together well with the chopped tomatoes (not in a blender). Transfer to a saucepan and heat through. Check the seasoning. When the pasta is cooked, drain it well and tip it into a warmed serving bowl. Lightly mix in the sauce, garnish with olives and serve immediately.

NOTE

✦ *Depending upon what you have available you can expand this dish to suit your appetite. Chunks of lightly cooked white fish would be a nice addition, as would mushrooms or stir-fried aubergine.*

Pasta with Double Mushrooms

CALORIES: **456**	PROTEIN: MEDIUM
TOTAL FAT: **16 g**	CARBOHYDRATE: ★★★
SATURATED FAT: **8.4 g**	FIBRE: **4 g**

MUSHROOMS and pasta have a special affinity. This recipe tastes nice and creamy but is, in fact, surprisingly low in fat.

1 × 30 g (1 oz) pack dried *porcini* mushrooms	juice of 1 lemon
300 g (10 oz) tagliatelle or tagliarini (dry weight)	150 g (5 oz) half-fat crème fraîche
1 tablespoon olive oil	75 g (3 oz) Fontina cheese, cut into cubes
300 g (10 oz) firm fresh mushrooms, sliced if large	salt and black pepper
1 clove garlic, chopped	1 tablespoon chopped fresh flat-leaved parsley
50 ml (2 fl oz) dry white wine	

Soak the dried mushrooms in hot water for 30 minutes, then drain, reserving the soaking liquid, and set aside. When the soaking time is up, cook the pasta in plenty of boiling salted water for about 8 minutes or until tender. Meanwhile, heat the oil in a non-stick frying pan, add the fresh mushrooms and garlic, and stir-fry over a high heat for about 2 minutes or until the mushrooms are lightly cooked. Add the dried mushrooms with 1 tablespoon of the soaking juice and the wine, and bring to the boil. Add the lemon juice and stir for 1 minute. Add the crème fraîche, cubed Fontina and some seasoning, and stir for a few seconds, by which time the pasta should be ready. Drain the pasta and tip it into a warmed serving bowl. Top with the mushroom sauce and stir to combine. Garnish with the chopped parsley and serve immediately.

Spinach and Ricotta Lasagne

SERVES 4

CALORIES: **424**	PROTEIN: HIGH
TOTAL FAT: **20 g**	CARBOHYDRATE: ★★
SATURATED FAT: **7.3 g**	FIBRE: **4.3 g**

LASAGNE is one of my absolute favourite winter dishes. It can be extremely high in fat – this version isn't quite saintly, but it is a lot less fatty than most versions, considering it contains cheese *and* cheese sauce!

600 g (22 oz) tender fresh spinach leaves	25 g (I oz) plain flour
175 g (6 oz) ricotta cheese	700 ml (24 fl oz) skimmed milk
1½ tablespoons pine nuts	50 g (2 oz) half-fat mature Cheddar cheese, grated
grated nutmeg	8 sheets 'no precook' lasagne (white)
salt and black pepper	3 tablespoons freshly grated Parmesan cheese
25 g (I oz) sunflower margarine	

Preheat the oven to 200°C/400°F/Gas Mark 6. Wilt the spinach in a little boiling water, then drain well, pressing out all surplus water. Leave to cool, then mix with the ricotta, pine nuts, nutmeg and seasoning. To make the cheese sauce, melt the margarine in a saucepan, stir in the flour and cook for 1–2 minutes, then remove from the heat and slowly add the milk, stirring all the time. Return to the heat and cook, stirring, until thickened and smooth. Add the Cheddar, stir and season to taste.

Spoon half the spinach mixture over the base of an ovenproof lasagne dish and cover with a third of the cheese sauce, then half the lasagne sheets. Cover these with the rest of the spinach mixture, top with the remaining lasagne sheets and pour over the rest of the sauce to coat evenly. Sprinkle the grated Parmesan on top and bake in the oven for 20–30 minutes or until the top is golden.

Tagliatelle with Cheese, Tomato and Greens

<u>SERVES 4</u>

CALORIES: 449	PROTEIN: HIGH
TOTAL FAT: 16 g	CARBOHYDRATE: ★★★
SATURATED FAT: 6.3 g	FIBRE: 4.9 g

SPINACH isn't the only leafy vegetable that goes well with pasta. Try a mixture in this recipe and see how good it is.

300 g (10 oz) mixed white and green tagliatelle (dry weight)	300 g (10 oz) mixed leaves of choice (see Note, below), sliced, torn or left whole as appropriate
2 tablespoons olive oil	3 medium tomatoes, de-seeded and chopped
I medium onion, finely chopped	6 cm (2½ inch) log medium-fat goat's cheese, diced
I clove garlic, chopped	(approx 200 g/7 oz)

Cook the pasta in plenty of lightly salted boiling water for about 8 minutes or until just tender. Meanwhile, heat half the oil in a non-stick frying pan and sauté the onion over a lowish heat for about 10 minutes or until soft. Add the garlic and stir for 1 minute, turning the heat up slightly. Add the rest of the oil, turn the heat up a little again, and stir-fry the leaves until well wilted. Add the chopped tomatoes, stir well, lower the heat and cook for 1–2 minutes. Meanwhile, drain the pasta, tip into a warmed serving bowl and keep warm. When the sauce is ready, pour it over the pasta and mix lightly. Add the goat's cheese before serving, stirring it in to combine.

NOTE

✦ *Leaves that are good in this dish are finely sliced chard, spring greens, radicchio or pak choi; sorrel, rocket, lovage or basil leaves (left whole if picked small, otherwise torn) used in slightly less quantity; or, of course, spinach!*

Pasta with Walnut Pesto

SERVES 4

CALORIES: **433**	PROTEIN: MEDIUM
TOTAL FAT: **19 g**	CARBOHYDRATE: ★★
SATURATED FAT: **2.8 g**	FIBRE: **2.8 g**

NUTS add protein to your pasta dish and, because they are high in oil, coat the pasta strands well.

60 g (2½ oz) walnuts	2 tablespoons extra-virgin olive oil
I large clove garlic	300 g (10 oz) spaghettini or spaghetti (dry weight)
sea salt and black pepper	2 tablespoons freshly grated Parmesan cheese
2 tablespoons chopped fresh flat-leaved parsley	

Using a pestle and mortar or an electric blender, blend together the walnuts, garlic, a little sea salt and the parsley, gradually adding the olive oil until you have a thick paste. Add black pepper to taste. Cook the pasta in plenty of lightly salted boiling water for about 8 minutes or until just tender. Drain the pasta, reserving 2 tablespoons of the cooking water. Mix the reserved water thoroughly into the walnut pesto. Tip the pasta into warmed serving bowls and toss with the pesto. Sprinkle the cheese over before serving.

Fusilli with Salmon and Leek

SERVES 4

CALORIES: 557	PROTEIN: HIGH
TOTAL FAT: 22 g	CARBOHYDRATE: ★★
SATURATED FAT: 7.6 g	FIBRE: 5.2 g

BECAUSE the fish and vegetables in this recipe aren't cooked in fat, we can afford to add a little in the form of delicious crème fraîche, making an easy luxury dish.

I stick celery, cut into julienne strips	I small avocado
2 medium carrots, cut into julienne strips	I tablespoon lemon juice
I medium leek, cut into julienne strips	salt and black pepper
300 g (10 oz) salmon fillet, skinned and cubed	300 g (10 oz) fusilli (dry weight)
100 ml (3½ fl oz) vegetable stock	I tablespoon chopped fresh dill
200 g (7 oz) half-fat crème fraîche	

Place the vegetable strips and the chunks of salmon in a pan, pour over the vegetable stock, and poach gently for 4–5 minutes or until everything is just cooked (the vegetables should still have some bite). Drain, reserving 1 tablespoon of the stock. Meanwhile, put the crème fraîche in a bowl. Halve, stone, peel and chop the avocado and add it to the crème fraîche with the lemon juice, seasoning and the reserved stock. Beat well to combine to a rich sauce. Cook the pasta in plenty of lightly salted boiling water for about 10 minutes or until just tender. Drain well and toss with the cream sauce. Serve with the salmon and vegetables on top, garnished with dill.

NOTE
✦ *If you can't get fresh dill, use parsley instead.*

*S*paghetti with Anchovies and Fried Herb Breadcrumbs

<u>SERVES 4</u>

CALORIES: **548**	PROTEIN: MEDIUM
TOTAL FAT: **24 g**	CARBOHYDRATE: ★★
SATURATED FAT: **3.8 g**	FIBRE: **2.7 g**

PASTA garnished with crispy fried breadcrumbs is absolutely gorgeous and not as wicked as it sounds. Try this!

300 g (10 oz) spaghetti (dry weight)	2 teaspoons chopped fresh oregano
100 ml (3½ fl oz) olive oil	2 teaspoons chopped fresh parsley
3 cloves garlic, lightly crushed	50 g (2 oz) can anchovies, drained and each
75 g (3 oz) slightly stale breadcrumbs from a good-	anchovy chopped into four
quality rustic white loaf	2 tablespoons freshly grated Parmesan cheese
2 teaspoons chopped fresh thyme	black pepper

Cook the pasta in plenty of lightly salted boiling water for about 10 minutes or until just tender. Meanwhile, pour the oil into a non-stick frying pan, add the garlic and sauté very gently for a few minutes, stirring the garlic around to flavour the oil well. Don't let the garlic brown too much; it should not turn anything deeper than golden. Remove the garlic from the oil and discard. Add the crumbs to the oil and stir well, cooking until they turn golden. Add the herbs and stir again. Transfer the crumbs to absorbent kitchen paper and pat well.

Drain the pasta and tip it into a warmed serving bowl. Add the anchovies, Parmesan and black pepper, and toss together. Sprinkle the fried crumbs over and serve immediately.

Macaroni Gratin with Aubergines and Tomatoes

SERVES 4

CALORIES: 469	PROTEIN: MEDIUM
TOTAL FAT: 16 g	CARBOHYDRATE: ★★★
SATURATED FAT: 2.9 g	FIBRE: 7.6 g

THIS is perhaps my favourite pasta dish in this book. Enough said!

200 g (7 oz) macaroni	2 cloves garlic, crushed
1 large or 2 small aubergines (approx 400 g/14 oz total weight)	250 ml (8 fl oz) passata
	1 rounded tablespoon sundried tomato paste
1 large red onion, cut into thin wedges	a good handful fresh basil leaves, chopped or torn
1 yellow pepper, de-seeded and sliced	250 ml (8 fl oz) ready-made white sauce for
2 tablespoons olive oil	lasagne (see Note, below)
salt and black pepper	1 half-fat mozzarella cheese (150 g/5 oz) in brine,
3 large tomatoes, halved, de-seeded and quartered	drained

Cook the macaroni in plenty of lightly salted boiling water for about 10 minutes or until just tender. Drain and set aside. Preheat the oven to 200°C/400°F/Gas Mark 6. Slice the aubergine(s) into 1 cm (½ inch) slices and halve. Lay them on a large baking tray. Add the onion pieces and the yellow pepper, drizzle over the oil and make sure everything is well coated, using your hands if necessary. Sprinkle on some salt and pepper and bake in the oven for 20 minutes. Add the tomatoes and garlic to the tray, tucking the garlic well in so it doesn't burn, and cook for a further 10–15 minutes until everything is soft and golden. Meanwhile, in a large bowl, mix the passata with the sundried tomato paste, the basil and some extra salt and pepper.

When the baked vegetables are ready, tip them into the passata mixture and combine well. Add the drained macaroni and mix again. Tip everything into a suitable shallow ovenproof dish, e.g. a lasagne dish, smooth down and pour the white sauce over evenly to cover (this will be a very thin layer of sauce). Finally, slice the mozzarella into thin rounds and place evenly over the top of the sauce. Return to the oven and bake for 20 minutes or until the top is golden.

NOTES AND TIPS
✦ *Penne or rigatoni would do as well as the macaroni.*
✦ *You can make your own white sauce (using skimmed milk) if you want to but there are some good ready-made lasagne sauces available from most large supermarkets.*

Pasta Primavera

SERVES 4

CALORIES: 342	PROTEIN: MEDIUM
TOTAL FAT: 6.3 g	CARBOHYDRATE: ★★★
SATURATED FAT: 1.8 g	FIBRE: 5.1 g

A HEALTHY and quick pasta dish, ideal for a summer supper.

300 g (10 oz) rigatoni or conchiglie	2 carrots, finely diced
1 tablespoon olive oil	1 medium courgette, halved lengthways and sliced
6 spring onions, chopped	50 g (2 oz) French beans, topped and tailed
1 medium leek, cut into thin rounds	$\frac{1}{2} \times$ 400 g (14 oz) can chopped tomatoes
100 g (3½ oz) small mushrooms	salt and black pepper
2 cloves garlic, well crushed	1 tablespoon half-fat crème fraîche

Cook the pasta in plenty of lightly salted boiling water for about 10 minutes or until just tender. Meanwhile, heat the olive oil in a frying pan and sauté the spring onions and leek for a few minutes or until just soft. Add the mushrooms and garlic and stir for a minute or two more. While this is happening, steam the carrots, courgette and French beans in a steamer or boil in a very little water until just tender. Refresh under running cold water, drain, and add to the other vegetables in the frying pan along with the chopped tomatoes and seasoning. Stir everything in well and heat through for a minute or two. When the pasta is ready, drain well and tip into a warmed serving bowl. Stir the crème fraîche into the vegetable mixture, toss with the pasta and serve immediately.

Tagliatelle with Calabrese and Sardines

SERVES 4

CALORIES: 562	PROTEIN: HIGH
TOTAL FAT: 23 g	CARBOHYDRATE: ★★
SATURATED FAT: 3.3 g	FIBRE: 4 g

SARDINES with some sweet sultanas and pine nuts make a great combination for a pasta sauce. Even if you think you won't like it, give it a try – it really is very good.

300 g (10 oz) green and white tagliatelle	2 × 120 g (4½ oz) can sardines in oil, well drained
2 tablespoons sultanas	2 tablespoons pine nuts
175 g (6 oz) calabrese, cut into small florets	1 tablespoon sundried tomato paste
2 tablespoons olive oil	2 tablespoons ready-made croûtons (see Note,
2 cloves garlic, crushed	below), crushed

Cook the tagliatelle in plenty of lightly salted boiling water for about 10 minutes or until just tender, adding the sultanas for the last minute of cooking time. Meanwhile, blanch the calabrese in a little boiling water and drain well. Heat the oil in a non-stick frying pan, add the calabrese and stir-fry for a few minutes until just tender. Add the garlic and stir for another minute. Take the bones out of the sardines and cut each into three, then add to the pan with the pine nuts, sundried tomato paste and 1 tablespoon water. Stir and heat through. Drain the pasta and sultanas and toss with the calabrese sauce. Serve with the crushed croûtons sprinkled over.

NOTES AND TIPS

✦ *You can make your own croûtons (see page 62) if you like. If using ready-made ones, crush in between foil using a rolling pin, or grind briefly in an electric mill. Alternatively, you could use a half quantity of fried breadcrumbs (see page 69) instead of the croûtons, which would increase the fat content of the dish somewhat. Omit the herbs if using that recipe.*

✦ *You can use fresh sardines instead of canned, in which case use eight whole sardines, and grill before boning and dicing.*

Papardelle with Peppers

SERVES 4

CALORIES: 357	PROTEIN: MEDIUM
TOTAL FAT: 7.9 g	CARBOHYDRATE: ★★★
SATURATED FAT: 1.1 g	FIBRE: 4.6 g

THIS is a very pretty dish; perhaps one to serve when friends come to supper.

1½ tablespoons olive oil	3 tablespoons red wine
1 large or 2 small red onions, sliced	½ × 400 g (14 oz) can chopped tomatoes
2 red peppers, de-seeded and sliced	salt and black pepper
1 clove garlic, chopped	1 tablespoon chopped fresh oregano
16 stoned black olives, halved	300 g (10 oz) papardelle

Heat the oil in a non-stick frying pan and sauté the onion, peppers and garlic for a few minutes, stirring from time to time, until soft and just turning golden. Stir in the remaining ingredients, except the pasta, and simmer for 10–15 minutes or until the peppers are tender and you have a rich sauce. Meanwhile, cook the pasta in plenty of lightly salted boiling water for about 10 minutes or until just tender. Drain and combine with the pepper sauce.

CHAPTER SIX

RICE AND GRAINS

Having sung the praises of pasta in the previous chapter, now I have reached the grains section, I realise that I am just as passionate about *them* – especially rice and couscous (which, as I've already mentioned, is a form of pasta, and appears in several recipes throughout this book). Some people dream of chocolate, others of carrot cake – I dream of great big steaming mounds of basmati rice in a succulent biryani, or platefuls of delicate and fluffy couscous, topped with delicious tomato-flavoured roast vegetables . . . mmm!

One of the best things about grains, though, is that they are all really good for your body as well as your soul. Rice, oats, barley, rye and wheat, and all the less well-known grains just becoming popular, are all nutritionally beyond reproach. They are complex carbohydrates and high in starch, vitamins, minerals and fibre – though, it is true, the processed grains such as white rice and pearl barley contain fewer vitamins and minerals, and less fibre than the whole grain varieties. Grains are low in fat, and each has its own specific benefits. Oats, for instance, are high in soluble fibre, which is the type of fibre that helps to reduce blood cholesterol if eaten regularly. Brown rice is a rich source of B vitamins and zinc.

Try to include a variety of grains as a large part of your main meal at least once or twice a week. Use them in salads, soups and side dishes; make pilafs, curries, paellas and risottos; stuff vegetables with any of the grains (leftovers are good used up this way) mixed with other vegetables, bake and serve with a tomato sauce; make stuffings for fish (and poultry if you ever eat it) – the jambalaya, biryani and pilaf recipes in this chapter all make good stuffings.

The other blessing of grains, apart from their low cost, is that they will store well in a cool, dry larder for quite a long time, so it is worth stocking up on a selection. I like to keep several types of rice – basmati, Thai fragrant, brown, wild, risotto, red and even one or two packets of the commercial 'speciality rices' such as pilau and saffron rice (good for quick meals). If I could be bothered with making sushi, I would also keep Japanese rice, but I'm just not that sort of cook – perhaps you are. I also have bulghar wheat, couscous, pearl barley, pot barley (i.e. barley with its seed still intact) and wheat berries (sometime sold as spelt). You can also buy packs of mixed grains, which are ideal for casseroles, soups and stews.

Grains marry very well with pulses (if you are vegan or vegetarian, this combination provides 'complete protein' in the same meal) and with nuts and seeds. You'll find more ideas on using grain, therefore, in the pulses chapter which begins on page 85.

Lastly, a word on cooking grains. Most packs that you buy will have cooking instructions on them, and I recommend following these rather than the general advice given here or in other cookery books, as even the same type of grain varies from country of origin to country of origin, and according to age, storage, preservation or processing methods, time of year harvested, and so on. Having said that, I do find that some instructions for cooking rice result in very watery, tasteless rice. In my experience, rice (when it is to be served as a side dish as you would potatoes, pasta, noodles, etc., or when needed pre-cooked for a recipe) is best cooked by the 'absorption' method, i.e. cooked in a limited amount of water (or stock) that will be fully absorbed by the end of the cooking time, no draining should be necessary. This means using a good-quality heavy saucepan with a tight-fitting lid, over a low heat, perhaps adding a little extra liquid towards the end of cooking if the rice has dried before it is tender, and finally, fluffing it through with a fork before using. For basmati rice, the king of rices, you need approximately 2.6 times as much liquid as you have rice, by weight. (You may need a little more.)

My final tip on the subject of grains is that cooked rice freezes quite well, so never throw leftovers away. (It doesn't last long in the fridge, though – even covered and well chilled, you should only keep it for a day or two before using it up. This is why freezing is such a good idea.)

Jambalaya

SERVES 4

CALORIES: 480	PROTEIN: HIGH
TOTAL FAT: 11 g	CARBOHYDRATE: ★★★
SATURATED FAT: 1 g	FIBRE: 3 g

JAMBALAYA is typical of the American creole style of cookery, so, of course, it's going to be hot! It is usually made with meat as well as vegetables and fish, but I found that vegetarian sausage mix worked very well in this recipe. You could leave it out if you want a lighter dish, or use chunks of chicken instead, if you eat poultry.

2 tablespoons corn oil	1 clove garlic, chopped
1 large onion, sliced	300 g (10 oz) basmati rice (dry weight)
1 green pepper, de-seeded and chopped	900 ml (1½ pints) vegetable stock
1 red pepper, de-seeded and chopped	½ × 400 g (14 oz) can chopped tomatoes
4 tablespoons vegetarian sausage mix (optional)	12 large peeled prawns *or* 175 g (6 oz) cubed Quorn
1 rounded teaspoon paprika	(see page 105)
2 hot red chillies, de-seeded and chopped (see Note, below)	

Heat the oil in a large non-stick frying pan or paella pan and sauté the onion and peppers over a medium high heat for about 10 minutes or until soft, stirring frequently. Add the sausage mix, if using, turn the heat up a little and stir until lightly browned. Add the paprika, chillies and garlic and stir for another minute, then tip in the rice, stir well, and add the stock and tomatoes. Bring to a simmer and simmer gently for 20 minutes or until almost all the stock has been absorbed and the rice is tender. Add the prawns or vegetable protein for the last 5 minutes of cooking.

NOTE
✦ *Adjust the amount of chilli according to your own taste and how hot the actual chillies are. Ask the vendor if you are unsure but, generally speaking, the larger chillies are the milder ones — it is the little, thin, pointed ones that are the killers!*

Spinach and Pine Nut Risotto

SERVES 4

CALORIES: 530	PROTEIN: MEDIUM
TOTAL FAT: 22 g	CARBOHYDRATE: ★★★
SATURATED FAT: 5.5 g	FIBRE: 3.8 g

MY favourite risottos are those flavoured with real saffron, a style that comes from Milan. You can now buy good-quality risotto rice 'Milanese', which means it is ready-flavoured with saffron to save you the trouble.

500 g (18 oz) prepared fresh spinach, baby leaves if possible	pinch of grated nutmeg
15 g (½ oz) butter	about 900 ml (1½ pints) vegetable stock
1 tablespoon olive oil	1 tablespoon ready-made basil pesto, preferably fresh (not from a jar)
1 medium onion, finely chopped	50 g (2 oz) pine nuts, toasted
1 clove garlic, chopped	salt and black pepper
300 g (10 oz) saffron risotto rice (dry weight)	30 g (1¼ oz) Parmesan cheese

Cook the spinach in a very little boiling water until wilted, stirring from time to time to hasten the process. Drain thoroughly and pat dry with absorbent kitchen paper. Chop the spinach roughly and set aside. Heat the butter and oil together in a non-stick risotto pan or large frying pan and sauté the onion for about 5 minutes or until soft, adding the garlic towards the end of the cooking time. Add the rice and stir for a minute, then add the nutmeg and stir again. Pour in a quarter of the stock and bring to a gentle simmer. Simmer, stirring from time to time, until the stock has been absorbed. Add another quarter of the stock and simmer again until absorbed, then repeat until all the stock is used up or the rice is tender and creamy. About 5 minutes before you estimate the risotto will be cooked, add the spinach, pesto and pine nuts, and stir in gently. Season with a little salt and plenty of black pepper. Serve topped with shavings of Parmesan.

NOTES AND TIPS
✦ *A similar risotto can be made using asparagus tips instead of spinach. Omit the pine nuts and add an extra 30 g (1¼ oz) cheese.*
✦ *If you can't get saffron risotto rice, use plain risotto rice and add a pinch or two of saffron just before you add the spinach.*

Stuffed Vine Leaves with Egg and Lemon Sauce

<u>SERVES 4</u>

CALORIES: 252	PROTEIN: MEDIUM
TOTAL FAT: 10 g	CARBOHYDRATE: ★★★
SATURATED FAT: 1.7 g	FIBRE: 2 g

THIS simple dish from Greece is one of my favourites. I think it is the smooth yet sharp tang of the 'avgolemono' sauce that makes it such a winner, though you can serve the stuffed leaves on their own as a lovely starter or buffet dish, just with some squeezed lemon juice, if you prefer.

40 vine leaves, prepacked in brine (see Note, below)	2 tablespoons finely chopped fresh mint
1 tablespoon olive oil	salt and black pepper
1 medium onion, finely chopped	350 ml (11 fl oz) cold vegetable stock
400 g (14 oz) cooked long grain white rice	2 medium free-range eggs
2 tablespoons pine nuts	juice of 2 lemons

Rinse the vine leaves, handling them carefully, and put them between layers of absorbent kitchen paper to dry. Heat the oil in a frying pan and sauté the onion for about 5 minutes or until soft and just turning golden. Stir the rice, pine nuts, mint and seasoning into the pan and combine well with the onion. Remove from the heat.

Preheat the oven to 190°C/375°F/Gas Mark 5. Spread one vine leaf flat in front of you and spoon a little of the rice stuffing on to the leaf just above the stalk. Roll up the leaf, tucking the ends underneath to form a small roll. Repeat until all the leaves are stuffed. Arrange the stuffed leaves tightly in a single layer, neat sides uppermost, in a suitably sized ovenproof dish. Pour about 100 ml (3½ fl oz) vegetable stock over the leaves, cover and bake in the oven for 30 minutes.

Meanwhile, beat the eggs in a jug. Add the lemon juice and beat in well. Add the remaining stock and beat again. When the vine leaves are nearly ready, pour the egg mixture into a saucepan and heat very gently, stirring, until the sauce thickens (it won't be very thick). Take care not to 'cook' the eggs by using too high a heat. At this stage you can add some of the stock from the baking dish if you like, which will have taken some flavour from the stuffed leaves. Remove the vine leaves from their dish using a slotted spatula and serve with the egg and lemon sauce poured over.

NOTES AND TIPS

♦ *Prepacked vine leaves are widely available at health food stores, specialist Greek shops and major supermarkets. If you can't find any, make the same dish using tender blanched cabbage leaves.*

♦ *If you're worried about the egg sauce (which, admittedly, can be tricky), simply make a fairly thin savoury white sauce using skimmed milk and add some lemon juice to it, beating in well.*

Chinese-Style Rice and Eggs

<u>SERVES 4</u>

CALORIES: 271	PROTEIN: HIGH
TOTAL FAT: 13 g	CARBOHYDRATE: ★★
SATURATED FAT: 4.1 g	FIBRE: 2.7 g

I LOVE special Chinese fried rice with its tasty chopped omelette. This is a variation, turned into a hearty supper with the addition of extra vegetables.

4 medium free-range eggs	2 small courgettes, thinly sliced
salt and black pepper	1 red pepper, de-seeded and chopped
10 g (¼ oz) butter	100 g (3½ oz) well-rinsed shredded seaweed (see
1 tablespoon chopped fresh coriander	Note, below) or spring greens
1½ tablespoons groundnut oil	300 g (10 oz) cooked basmati rice
1 teaspoon grated fresh ginger	100 g (3½ oz) beansprouts
1 clove garlic, crushed	1 tablespoon light soy sauce
6 spring onions, chopped	2 teaspoons chilli sauce

First make the omelette: beat the eggs together with 1 tablespoon cold water, a pinch of salt and some black pepper. Heat the butter in an omelette pan and, when very hot, add the eggs. To help the egg cook, pull the set edges towards the centre of the pan with a spatula, tipping the pan if necessary to encourage the raw egg to run from the top to the edges to cook. When the underside is cooked and the top is still slightly runny, sprinkle the chopped coriander over and, using the spatula, fold up into a plump omelette. Turn out on to a flat plate and leave for a minute to cool before slicing crossways.

Heat the oil in a wok or large frying pan and add the ginger, garlic, spring onions, courgettes and red pepper. Stir-fry for a few minutes or until the vegetables are slightly soft. Add the seaweed or greens and stir-fry for another minute. Add the rice and beansprouts with the soy and chilli sauces, and stir gently for 2 minutes, adding a little water or vegetable stock if the rice looks like sticking. Finally, add the omelette slices and serve.

NOTE

✦ *Dulse, wakami or kombu are three popular types of seaweed. An easy way to buy them is in dried form – you soak to reconstitute the seaweed, then rinse well and pat dry with absorbent kitchen paper. It is then ready to use in the recipe above.*

Coulibiac Filo Tarts

SERVES 4

CALORIES: 482	PROTEIN: HIGH
TOTAL FAT: 20 g	CARBOHYDRATE: ★
SATURATED FAT: 3.6 g	FIBRE: 2.4 g

THIS is a great dinner–party dish which is less calorific by far than the traditional salmon coulibiac which uses masses of puff pastry and butter.

4 sheets filo pastry	100 g (3½ oz) button mushrooms, sliced
low-fat cooking spray	300 g (10 oz) cooked white and wild rice
100 g (3½ oz) calabrese	2 medium free-range eggs, hard-boiled and
1 tablespoon corn oil	chopped
1 medium onion, finely chopped	juice of 1 lemon
450 g (1 lb) salmon fillet, skinned and cut into	1 tablespoon chopped fresh parsley or dill
small chunks	salt and black pepper

Preheat the oven to 190°C/375°F/Gas Mark 5. Cut the filo sheets into four squares each and arrange in layers in four patty tins, spraying both sides of each square with low-fat spray. Smooth the layers down into the tins nicely to make four pretty tart cases, and bake in the oven for about 15 minutes or until lightly golden.

While the pastry is cooking, cut the calabrese into small florets and boil in lightly salted water for a few minutes until barely tender. Drain and refresh in cold water. Meanwhile, heat the oil in a non-stick frying pan and sauté the onion for about 10 minutes or until soft and just turning golden, stirring occasionally and adding the salmon for the last 3 minutes of cooking. Add the mushrooms and calabrese and stir for a minute or two, then add the rice, eggs, lemon juice, herbs and seasoning and stir gently. By this time the filo cases should be ready; remove them from the oven and fill with the rice mixture. Serve at once.

NOTES AND TIPS
✦ *Make the dish in advance, if you like, and reheat the cases gently in a warm oven while reheating the filling in a low microwave (be very careful not to overheat or the salmon will dry out).*
✦ *Serve with green salad.*

Vegetable Biryani

SERVES 4

CALORIES: 485	PROTEIN: MEDIUM
TOTAL FAT: 11 g	CARBOHYDRATE: ★★★
SATURATED FAT: 1.8 g	FIBRE: 4.8 g

THIS is a good dish for a supper with friends when you want everything to be nice and relaxed. It is very forgiving and will happily keep warm, in a covered dish, in the oven while you chat.

2 small aubergines (about 400 g/14 oz total weight)	1 tablespoon mild curry paste
	100 g (3½ oz) canned chopped tomatoes
2 tablespoons olive or groundnut oil	300 g (10 oz) quick-cook brown rice
1 large onion, finely chopped	900 ml (1½ pints) vegetable stock
2 cloves garlic, chopped	200 g (7 oz) waxy new potatoes, cooked
pinch of sugar	50 g (2 oz) sultanas
1 rounded teaspoon freshly ground coriander seed	salt and black pepper
1 rounded teaspoon freshly ground cumin	250 g (9 oz) natural bio yogurt

Cut the aubergines into small bite-sized cubes. Bring a pan of lightly salted water to the boil, add the aubergine cubes, and boil for a few minutes or until soft. Drain and pat dry on absorbent kitchen paper, then set aside. Heat the oil in a large non-stick frying pan or paella pan and sauté the onion for about 5 minutes or until soft, stirring from time to time. Add the garlic towards the end of this time, along with the sugar, spices and curry paste. Stir for a minute or two, then add the tomatoes, rice and stock, stir again and bring to a simmer. After 15 minutes, add the aubergines, potatoes and sultanas, and simmer for a further 10 minutes or until most of the stock has been absorbed and the rice and vegetables are tender. Season to taste and stir in the yogurt before serving.

NOTE
✦ *You can add some flaked toasted almonds to the dish if you like, as a garnish, or stir in extra chopped vegetables to suit yourself. You can also try the same recipe using spelt (wheat berries).*

Gratin of Polenta and Mediterranean Vegetables

SERVES 4

CALORIES: **378**	PROTEIN: HIGH
TOTAL FAT: 19 g	CARBOHYDRATE: ★★
SATURATED FAT: 9.5 g	FIBRE: 5.1 g

POLENTA (an Italian dish made from cornmeal) isn't incredibly appetising unless you jazz it up with some cheese and a little butter, which turns it into a feast that is fit for kings but rather high in fat, so it needs teaming with lots of low-fat, high-fibre vegetables to turn it into a healthy dish overall. This recipe is ideal.

low-fat cooking spray	1 tablespoon chopped fresh oregano
2 good-sized courgettes	100 ml (3½ fl oz) passata
1 large aubergine	100 g (3½ oz) half-fat mozzarella cheese
2 red peppers, de-seeded	600 ml (1 pint) vegetable stock
1 red onion	100 g (3½ oz) quick-cook polenta
1 tablespoon olive oil	100 g (3½ oz) Gruyère cheese
salt and black pepper	25 g (1 oz) butter
2 cloves garlic, crushed	

Preheat the oven to 190°C/375°F/Gas Mark 5. Spray a large baking tray with low-fat cooking spray. Cut all the vegetables into large chunks or slices, arrange on the baking tray, brush with the olive oil, and season. Bake in the oven for 30 minutes or until turning golden and tender. When ready, turn into a large gratin dish and scatter the crushed garlic and oregano around. Pour the passata over. Slice the mozzarella (unless you are using the ready-grated kind) and lay it over the top.

Heat the stock in a saucepan and, when it is boiling, add the polenta, stirring all the time. Cook for a few minutes until you have a thick paste, then remove from the heat and stir in the Gruyère and butter with some seasoning. Spoon this mixture over the top of the cheese and vegetables, spreading it evenly. Return the dish to the hot oven and bake for 20 minutes or until the polenta topping is golden.

Barley Bake

SERVES 4

CALORIES: 451	PROTEIN: LOW
TOTAL FAT: 13 g	CARBOHYDRATE: ★★★
SATURATED FAT: 3.6 g	FIBRE: 4.4 g

THIS is a kind of vegetarian cottage pie. Pearl barley makes a nice, creamy sauce but you could use wheat grains or pot barley instead, or even millet.

175 g (6 oz) pearl barley	I clove garlic, chopped
600 g (22 oz) floury potatoes	2 medium carrots, chopped
50 ml (2 fl oz) skimmed milk	I tablespoon plain flour
2 tablespoons olive oil	500 ml (18 fl oz) vegetable stock
50 g (2 oz) Gruyère cheese, grated	I tablespoon Worcestershire sauce
salt and black pepper	2 teaspoons sundried tomato paste
I large onion, finely chopped	100 g (3½ oz) field or chestnut mushrooms

Put the pearl barley in a saucepan and cover with water. Bring to the boil, then lower the heat and simmer for 30 minutes. Drain, reserving the cooking liquid. Meanwhile, peel the potatoes, cut into chunks, and cook in lightly salted boiling water for 15–20 minutes until tender. Drain and mash with the skimmed milk, half the olive oil, the cheese and some seasoning. Set aside.

Heat the remaining olive oil in a non-stick frying pan and sauté the onion for about 5 minutes or until soft. Add the garlic and carrots and stir for 1 minute, then stir in the flour and cook for 1 minute. Add the stock with the reserved barley cooking water, stirring all the time, then add the Worcestershire sauce and tomato paste. Bring to a simmer, add the mushrooms, cover and cook for 20 minutes. Season to taste. Pour into an ovenproof dish and smooth the mashed potato over the top. Bake in the oven at 200°C/400°F/Gas Mark 6, or place under a hot grill until the top is golden, then serve.

NOTES
+ *Serve with plenty of green vegetables.*
+ *As this dish is low in protein, make sure you get at least one high protein meal during the day. Alternatively, add extra cheese to the potatoes, not forgetting this will also add fat (and calories) to the dish.*

CHAPTER SEVEN

PULSES

All the members of the large and diverse pulse family – peas, beans and lentils – are important components of a non-meat diet because they are excellent sources of low-fat protein. For vegans, who eat no dairy produce, and for any non-meat eater trying to reduce fat in the diet, they are virtually indispensable. Pulses also contain (in varying amounts) complex carbohydrate, soluble and insoluble fibre, and plenty of vitamins and minerals. They are also *very* filling, so are ideal for hungry slimmers.

No two varieties of dried pulse taste the same or have the same texture, and most have different cooking properties. For example, brown lentils, kidney beans, black beans and Egyptian brown beans are all ideal for people who like a rich, meaty taste and strong texture; cannellini and flageolet beans are delicate and light to eat; butter beans and lima beans are meltingly soft and sweet; and so on . . .

There are no limits to their uses – for main meals, soups and stews, pies, pâtés, dips, spreads, bakes, curries, stir-fries. There isn't room here to list all the best uses of every pulse, but if the recipes in this chapter get you more interested in bean cuisine, there are several good books available that are devoted to beans alone.

There are so many different kinds of pulses that it isn't hard to find at least some that you really love, which is why it is difficult to understand why some of us make no use of peas, beans and lentils at all. The most common excuse is that they cause flatulence, but if you cook them properly, chew them thoroughly and add them to your diet gradually, in slowly increasing amounts, this needn't be a problem. Another complaint I hear is that dried pulses take too long to cook and are often tough even after long cooking. The easy answer, of course, is to use canned ready-cooked beans. Nutritionally, these are just as good apart from the fact that many canned beans contain quite a lot of added salt, so if you are trying to watch your salt intake, read the can labels and choose beans canned in water rather than brine. If you do use beans preserved in brine, rinse them well before use.

That said, there are times when dried beans are preferable (in slow-cooking casseroles, for instance) as well as being cheaper. Simply soak them for the length of time suggested on the pack (or overnight if no soaking time is given), drain, boil rapidly in fresh water for 10 minutes to eliminate toxins, and then use in your recipe, or simmer in more water, without salt which tends to toughen the beans, until they are tender. Season to taste once cooked. Simmering time will depend upon the type of beans and how long they have been stored. If you buy pulses in the autumn and they are new stock, they will be the new season's pulses and will not need as much soaking or cooking as ancient 'has beans'. If you've had trouble in the past with rock-hard pulses (most complaints seem to be about chick peas), it is time to buy new stock and have another go.

To make the most of dried pulses, you need to get into the habit of planning ahead, but there is one important exception to this: lentils and split peas need no soaking at all and can be tender and ready to eat after only half an hour's simmering. So if you like short-cuts, then lentils are definitely for you.

Lentil and Roasted Squash Gratin

SERVES 4

CALORIES: 367	PROTEIN: HIGH
TOTAL FAT: 15 g	CARBOHYDRATE: ★★
SATURATED FAT: 6 g	FIBRE: 7.9 g

THIS is an easy meal. All members of the pumpkin family are good partners for lentils but I prefer the denser tastier flesh of other winter squashes to that of pumpkins which can be a bit watery.

200 g (7 oz) green lentils	2 tablespoons olive oil
2 courgettes (preferably golden-skinned), halved lengthways then sliced	salt and black pepper
	2 teaspoons balsamic vinegar
1 small butternut squash, peeled, de-seeded and cut into small cubes	1 clove garlic, very finely chopped
	1 tablespoon finely chopped fresh coriander
1 mild onion, cut into 1 cm (½ inch) slices	100 g (3½ oz) Fontina cheese

Preheat the oven to 190°C/375°F/Gas Mark 5. Wash and drain the lentils.

Toss the courgette, squash and onion pieces in a bowl with half the olive oil and some seasoning, then spread out on a baking tray and roast in the oven for 25–30 minutes or until the pieces are tender and just turning golden.

Meanwhile, simmer the lentils in water for 30 minutes or until tender, then drain and transfer to a bowl. Combine the remaining olive oil with the vinegar, garlic and some seasoning. Pour over the lentils while they are still warm, and toss well. Add the roasted vegetables and coriander, and mix well, then spoon everything into a gratin dish and smooth out. Cut the cheese into thin slices, arrange on top and bake in the oven for 10 minutes or until the cheese is melted and golden.

NOTE
✦ *Serve with salad and crusty bread.*

Spicy Spinach, Chick Peas and Peppers

SERVES 4

CALORIES: 210	PROTEIN: HIGH
TOTAL FAT: 7.4 g	CARBOHYDRATE: ★★
SATURATED FAT: 0.9 g	FIBRE: 7.5 g

MANY pulses, particularly chick peas, need to be combined with something acidic to bring out their best flavour – lemon juice, tomatoes or, often, vinegar, as in this recipe.

I tablespoon olive oil	½ teaspoon freshly ground coriander
6 spring onions, finely chopped	I teaspoon Hungarian paprika
I clove garlic, chopped	500 g (18 oz) (drained weight) pre-cooked or
250 g (9 oz) baby spinach	canned chick peas (see Note, below)
150 g (5 oz) canned or bottled red peppers, well	I tablespoon white wine vinegar
drained and sliced	I tablespoon tomato purée
½ teaspoon freshly ground cumin	salt and black pepper

Heat the oil in a large non-stick frying pan and stir-fry the spring onions, garlic and spinach until the leaves are wilted. Add the red peppers and spices, and stir again for a minute, then add the remaining ingredients and stir for a few more minutes, adding a little water or vegetable stock if things look too dry (though this is a dry dish). Season to taste and serve.

NOTES AND TIPS
✦ *Serve with flat bread or rice.*
✦ *If using canned chick peas, two 400 g (14 oz) cans will provide 500 g (18 oz) drained chick peas.*

Ragu of Brown Lentils

SERVES 4

CALORIES: 301	PROTEIN: HIGH
TOTAL FAT: 11 g	CARBOHYDRATE: ★★
SATURATED FAT: 1.4 g	FIBRE: 7.5 g

HERE is an ideal recipe for use with pasta, a kind of no-meat bolognese sauce.

2 tablespoons olive oil	100 g (3½ oz) mushrooms, finely chopped
2 medium onions, finely chopped	100 g (3½ oz) carrot, chopped
175 g (6 oz) brown lentils	100 ml (3½ fl oz) vegetable stock
1 clove garlic, chopped	1 quantity Home-Made Tomato Sauce (see page 107)
1 stick celery, finely chopped	salt and black pepper

Heat the oil in a large non-stick frying pan and sauté the onions until soft and just turning golden. Add the lentils and garlic, stir for a minute, then add the rest of the ingredients, except the salt, bring to a simmer, cover and cook for about 30 minutes or until you have a rich sauce. (You may need to adjust the amount of stock you use slightly, depending upon the water content of the ingredients.) Season to taste.

NOTE
✦ *Serve on spaghetti or with rice or grilled polenta, spelt or couscous, plus a salad.*

Bean and Tomato Hotpot

SERVES 4

CALORIES: 354	PROTEIN: HIGH
TOTAL FAT: 7.3 g	CARBOHYDRATE: ★★★
SATURATED FAT: 1 g	FIBRE: 13 g

A SIMPLE winter dish; one that my whole family loves.

2 tablespoons corn oil	1 × 200 g (7 oz) can butter beans, well rinsed and
2 medium onions, sliced	drained
3 medium carrots, sliced	300 ml (½ pint) vegetable stock
2 sticks celery, diced	1 × 400 g (14 oz) can chopped tomatoes with
2 leeks, sliced	herbs
1 clove garlic, crushed	salt and black pepper
1 × 400 g (14 oz) can red kidney beans, well rinsed	700 g (1½ lb) potatoes, peeled and thinly sliced
and drained	

Preheat the oven to 180°C/350°F/Gas Mark 4. Heat the oil in a flameproof
casserole and sauté the onions for a few minutes, until slightly soft, then add
the carrots, celery and leeks, and sauté for a few more minutes, adding the
garlic for the last minute. Add the remaining ingredients, except the potatoes,
and mix well. Arrange the potato slices over the top to cover thoroughly and
season. Cover and bake in the oven for 1 hour, then remove the lid and bake,
uncovered, for a further 30 minutes.

NOTE

✦ *Serve with some green vegetables or a winter salad.*

OPPOSITE *Papardelle with Peppers (page 73) served with herb salad*

Spicy Mushrooms with Cannellini Beans

SERVES 4

CALORIES: 189	PROTEIN: HIGH
TOTAL FAT: 9.5 g	CARBOHYDRATE: ★★
SATURATED FAT: 1.4 g	FIBRE: 7.1 g

YOU can use borlotti, black–eye or brown beans in this dish, or even a mixture if you are feeling adventurous.

3 tablespoons light olive oil	400 g (14 oz) mixed mushrooms, chopped or torn,
2 medium onions, sliced	as necessary (see Note, below)
1 teaspoon crushed cumin seeds	1 × 400 g (14 oz) can cannellini beans, rinsed and
1 teaspoon ground coriander	drained
1 teaspoon ground turmeric	1 × 400 g (14 oz) can chopped tomatoes
½ teaspoon ground cinnamon	salt and black pepper
½ teaspoon chilli powder	2 tablespoons chopped fresh coriander

Heat the oil in a large non–stick frying pan and sauté the onions for 5 minutes, then add all the spices and sauté for 5 minutes more, stirring frequently. Add the mushrooms, stir for a minute, then add the beans and tomatoes. Simmer for 10 minutes, check the seasoning and add a little salt if necessary. Sprinkle over the coriander and serve.

NOTES AND TIPS

✦ *Mixed mushrooms can be any combination you like, although my favourites are brown caps (chestnut), shiitake and re-constituted porcini. Economy pack mushrooms won't produce such a rich flavour.*

✦ *Serve on a grain or with mashed potatoes or pasta and salad or greens.*

OPPOSITE *Mushroom and Sweetcorn Sizzle with Thai Flavours (page 101) served with noodles and accompanied by Herb Salad with Orange Vinaigrette (page 118)*

Lentil and Sweet Potato Curry

<u>SERVES 4</u>

CALORIES: 327	PROTEIN: HIGH
TOTAL FAT: 7.3 g	CARBOHYDRATE: ★★★
SATURATED FAT: 1.2 g	FIBRE: 7.6 g

A QUICK curry that looks great. Use orange-fleshed sweet potatoes, which are creamy and rich in beta-carotene, rather than the white-fleshed ones, although these will do at a pinch.

2 tablespoons corn or groundnut oil	1 teaspoon ground coriander
400 g (14 oz) sweet potatoes, cut into bite-sized chunks	400 g (14 oz) pre-cooked or canned brown or green lentils (about 130 g/4½ oz before cooking)
1 medium onion, finely chopped	250 g (9 oz) cooked old potatoes, cut into bite-sized chunks
1 clove garlic, chopped	
1 green chilli, chopped (see Note, below)	about 300 ml (½ pint) vegetable stock
1 teaspoon cumin seeds	salt and black pepper
½ teaspoon ground ginger	4 tablespoons natural low-fat bio yogurt (optional)

Heat the oil in a non-stick frying pan and, when hot, add the sweet potato chunks. Stir-fry over a high heat for a few minutes, until golden. Remove from the pan with a slotted spoon and set aside. Add the onion to the pan and stir for a few minutes to soften, then add the garlic, chilli and all the spices, and stir-fry for 1–2 minutes. Return the sweet potatoes to the pan with the lentils, potatoes, half the stock, and seasoning, and simmer for 30 minutes, adding extra stock once or twice if the curry gets too dry (there should only be a small amount of sauce). Check the seasoning, stir in the yogurt, if using, and serve.

NOTES AND TIPS

✦ *Serve with rice and/or chapatis, plus a cucumber salad.*
✦ *For a milder curry, discard the seeds when preparing the chilli. Always wash your hands thoroughly after preparing fresh chillies.*

Bean and Pasta Bake

SERVES 4

CALORIES: **388**	PROTEIN: HIGH
TOTAL FAT: **8.6 g**	CARBOHYDRATE: ★★★
SATURATED FAT: **1.2 g**	FIBRE: **9.6 g**

CHILDREN like this one — it is a good teatime treat for cold evenings.

175 g (6 oz) pasta shapes of choice	I tablespoon soft brown sugar
I tablespoon corn oil	I tablespoon lemon juice
I medium onion, finely chopped	salt and black pepper
I quantity Home-Made Tomato Sauce (see page 107)	400 g (14 oz) pre-cooked or canned haricot beans,
2 teaspoons mustard powder	drained (about 130 g/4½ oz before cooking)
2 teaspoons black treacle	

Preheat the oven to 150°C/300°F/Gas Mark 2. Cook the pasta in plenty of
lightly salted boiling water for about 12 minutes or until just tender. Drain
and set aside. Heat the oil in a flameproof casserole and sauté the onion for
about 5 minutes or until soft. Add the tomato sauce, mustard, treacle, sugar,
lemon juice and seasoning, and simmer for 1 minute. Stir in the cooked beans
and the pasta, plus a little water if the sauce seems a bit dry. Cover and bake in
the oven for 1½ hours, stirring once or twice and adding a little more water if
necessary. Check the seasoning and serve.

NOTE
✦ *Serve with salad and, if you or the children are very hungry, some crusty bread.*

Chilli Beans with Tortilla Crust

SERVES 4

CALORIES: **346**	PROTEIN: HIGH
TOTAL FAT: **11 g**	CARBOHYDRATE: ★★★
SATURATED FAT: **2.7 g**	FIBRE: **9.6 g**

THIS is a kind of chilli sans carne. The basic recipe can be used as a topping for rice instead, or for filling baked potatoes or pancakes.

1 tablespoon corn oil	500 g (18 oz) canned mixed pulses (see Note, below)
1 large onion, finely chopped	
1 large green pepper, de-seeded and chopped	1 × 400 g (14 oz) can chopped tomatoes
1 clove garlic, chopped	salt and black pepper
1 tablespoon paprika	80 g (3 oz) bag tortilla chips
2 teaspoons ground cumin	50 g (2 oz) half-fat Cheddar cheese, grated
1 red chilli, de-seeded and chopped	

Preheat the oven to 190°C/375°F/Gas Mark 5. Heat the oil in a large non-stick frying pan and sauté the onion and green pepper over a medium-high heat for 5–10 minutes or until turning golden. Add the garlic and spices, and stir-fry for 1 minute. Add the beans, tomatoes and seasoning, stir and simmer for 15 minutes or until you have a thick sauce. Pour the mixture into an ovenproof dish. Crush the tortillas lightly and sprinkle over the chilli beans, then top with the cheese. Bake in the oven for 15 minutes or until the top is golden.

NOTES AND TIPS
✦ *Serve with salad, and, if your diet can take the extra fat, with guacamole.*
✦ *Two 400 g (14 oz) cans mixed pulses will provide 500 g (18 oz) when drained.*

Aubergine and Lentil Gratin

SERVES 4

CALORIES: 320	PROTEIN: HIGH
TOTAL FAT: 9.1 g	CARBOHYDRATE: ★★
SATURATED FAT: 2.5 g	FIBRE: 11 g

I MAKE no apology for aubergines appearing in several of my recipes; they are infinitely useful, and always delicious.

2 medium aubergines	1 tablespoon chopped fresh coriander
1 tablespoon olive oil	500 g (18 oz) pre-cooked or canned brown or Puy
1 medium onion, thinly sliced	lentils (about 170 g/6 oz before cooking)
1 yellow pepper, de-seeded and sliced	salt and black pepper
1 clove garlic, crushed	1 tablespoon freshly grated Parmesan cheese
1 tablespoon sundried tomato paste	50 g (2 oz) half-fat mature Cheddar cheese, grated
350 ml (12 fl oz) passata	4 tablespoons slightly stale breadcrumbs

Preheat the oven to 190°C/375°F/Gas Mark 5. Slice the aubergines into 1 cm (½ inch) rounds and parboil in lightly salted water for 4 minutes. Drain and pat dry with absorbent kitchen paper. Heat the oil in a non-stick frying pan and sauté the onion and yellow pepper for 5–10 minutes or until soft and turning golden. Add the garlic and stir-fry for 1 minute. Mix the tomato paste with the passata, stir in the coriander and pour this into the frying pan with the lentils. Arrange half the aubergine slices in a layer in a gratin dish and pour on half the lentil mixture. Season, then repeat the layers, seasoning again. Mix the cheeses with the breadcrumbs and sprinkle over the top of the lentils. Bake in the oven for 40 minutes or until the topping is golden and the vegetables are tender.

Lentil Pie with Parsnip, Leek and Potato Topping

<u>SERVES 4</u>

CALORIES: **298**	PROTEIN: HIGH
TOTAL FAT: **6 g**	CARBOHYDRATE: ★★★
SATURATED FAT: **0.8 g**	FIBRE: **12 g**

A TASTY, inexpensive dish, ideal for a winter supper.

I tablespoon corn oil	I tablespoon tomato purée
I medium onion, sliced	400 g (14 oz) parsnips, diced
I large carrot, diced	400 g (14 oz) potatoes, peeled and diced
I tablespoon mild curry paste	I large leek, sliced
225 g (8 oz) mixed lentils	50 ml (2 fl oz) skimmed milk
250 ml (8 fl oz) salt-free vegetable stock	salt and black pepper
I × 400 g (14 oz) can chopped tomatoes with (optional) chilli	

Heat the oil in a large saucepan and sauté the onion for about 5 minutes or until soft. Add the carrot, curry paste and lentils, stir for a minute, then add the stock, tomatoes and tomato purée. Simmer for 30 minutes or until the lentils are tender. Meanwhile, boil the parsnips and potatoes in lightly salted water for about 20 minutes or until tender, and boil the leek in another pan for 5 minutes or until tender. Preheat the oven to 200°C/400°F/Gas Mark 6.

Drain the potatoes and parsnips, and the leek. Mash the potatoes and parsnips together with the skimmed milk and some seasoning, then stir in the leeks. Season the lentils to taste and spoon into an ovenproof dish. Top with the mash and bake in the oven for 15 minutes or until the topping is crisp.

NOTE
✦ *Serve with green vegetables.*

CHAPTER EIGHT

VEGETABLE MAIN COURSES

Y ou cannot have failed to notice that we are all being implored by health experts to 'eat up our greens' with a greater and greater sense of urgency. Apparently, seven out of ten children hate vegetables and two out of three adults never manage to eat their five portions of fruit and vegetables a day, as recommended by the UK Department of Health.

I am never quite sure why so many people find vegetables such a problem. With everywhere from supermarkets and cornershops to organic and pick-your-own farms stocking a wealth of interesting vegetables, surely there is something for everyone. Vegetables aren't necessarily expensive, and they are so colourful and gorgeous that a meal without them is very dull, to say the least.

For me, it is an easy step from a meal that includes lots of vegetables to a meal made solely, or almost so, from vegetables, and that's what the recipes in this chapter are all about. I have added extra protein to some dishes in the form of dairy produce or similar, but I find that vegetables can be satisfying without any such additions. Many vegetables do contain reasonable amounts of protein – potatoes, legumes, mushrooms, for instance – but of course that isn't their starring role within our diets: we need more vegetables because of the vitamins, minerals, fibre, carbohydrate and mysterious, health-giving 'phytochemicals' they contain. These 'added ingredients', which you can't get from a pill, may help prevent cancers, heart disease, ageing, and many other twenty-first-century problems. I hope that the recipes in this chapter will inspire you to try more 'mainly-veg' main meals. If you are short of time, don't fall back on the fish fingers: grill a tray of vegetables and serve with couscous, or stir-fry a selection and serve with noodles or rice.

I buy organic vegetables or grow my own. Not everyone is so lucky but please do make sure you buy the freshest, best-quality produce you can, which will make a huge difference to your finished dishes.

Creamy Vegetable Pie

<u>SERVES 6</u>

CALORIES: **238**	PROTEIN: MEDIUM
TOTAL FAT: **8.9 g**	CARBOHYDRATE: ★★★
SATURATED FAT: **4.2 g**	FIBRE: **4.5 g**

EVERY now and then we all enjoy something rich and creamy, with a good portion of crispy pastry on top. This fits the bill without being completely over the top as far as calories and fat are concerned.

2 medium leeks, sliced	40 g (1½ oz) butter
2 carrots, halved lengthways then sliced	I rounded tablespoon plain flour
I parsnip cut into small chunks	450 ml (¾ pint) skimmed milk, warmed
200 g (7 oz) butternut squash, peeled, de-seeded and cut into small chunks	salt and black pepper
I courgette, cut into small chunks	5 oblong sheets filo pastry
75 g (3 oz) yellow split peas, pre-cooked or canned, drained	I tablespoon olive oil

Parboil all the vegetables, except the split peas, in lightly salted boiling water for 5–7 minutes, drain and arrange in an ovenproof lasagne dish or similar. Spoon the cooked split peas around them. Heat the butter in a non-stick saucepan and, when melted and bubbling, add the flour. Stir well and cook over a medium heat for 2 minutes, stirring. Remove from the heat and slowly add the milk, stirring, to make a white sauce. When all the milk is in, season well and pour the sauce over the vegetables, mixing in a little.

Preheat the oven to 190°C/375°F/Gas Mark 5. Brush the filo pastry sheets lightly on both sides with olive oil, then arrange on top of the pie to form a crust. Crinkle the top sheet slightly before putting in the oven. Bake for 25 minutes or until golden.

NOTE
✦ *Serve with broccoli and green beans.*

Vegetable Sagu

SERVES 4

CALORIES: 194	PROTEIN: MEDIUM
TOTAL FAT: 4.2 g	CARBOHYDRATE: ★★★
SATURATED FAT: 0.6 g	FIBRE: 6.5 g

A SAGU is a hot vegetable curry. Vary the vegetables according to what is in season and what you like best, but potatoes and at least one other chunky vegetable should form a major part of the dish.

500 g (18 oz) potatoes, peeled and cubed	I teaspoon ground cardamom seeds
I medium aubergine, cubed	½ teaspoon ground cinnamon
I tablespoon corn oil	½ teaspoon ground black pepper
I large onion, finely chopped	I teaspoon ground coriander seeds
I clove garlic, crushed	I × 400 g (14 oz) can chopped tomatoes
I teaspoon cumin seeds	200 ml (7 fl oz) vegetable stock
I rounded teaspoon grated fresh ginger	100 g (3½ oz) green beans
I dried chilli, chopped	100 g (3½ oz) small peas

Parboil the potatoes and aubergine in lightly salted water for 5 minutes. Drain and set aside. Heat the oil in a large non-stick frying pan and stir-fry the onion, garlic and cumin seeds over a high heat for a few minutes or until the onion is turning golden and the cumin seeds are popping. Add the rest of the spices, turn the heat down and stir well for 1 minute. Add the rest of the ingredients, including the potatoes and aubergine, and stir well. Bring to a simmer, turn the heat down and cook for 30 minutes, uncovered, until everything is tender and the sauce is rich.

NOTE
✦ *Serve garnished with chopped fresh coriander if you like, with chapatis and/or rice.*

*S*tir-Fried Peppers with Rosti and Poached Eggs

SERVES 4

CALORIES: 342

TOTAL FAT: 15 g

SATURATED FAT: 2.8 g

PROTEIN: MEDIUM

CARBOHYDRATE: ★★

FIBRE: 6.2 g

IF you are short of time, you could serve the peppers and eggs on top of large slices of bruschetta – slices of country bread brushed with olive oil and garlic and toasted or baked lightly until golden.

600 g (22 oz) potatoes, unpeeled	I green pepper, de-seeded and sliced
salt and black pepper	2 red onions, sliced
3 tablespoons olive oil	2 cloves garlic, chopped
2 large red peppers, de-seeded and sliced	4 medium free-range eggs
I large yellow pepper, de-seeded and sliced	2 teaspoons chilli sauce

Parboil the potatoes in lightly salted water for 10 minutes. Drain and cool. Remove the skins and, using a coarse grater, grate the potatoes into a large bowl. Season well. Heat half the oil in a non-stick frying pan and add the potato, spreading it evenly and pressing down lightly. Cook over a medium heat, without stirring, for about 10 minutes or until the underside is browned. Place a plate upside-down over the potato and invert the pan so that the potato is brown-side-up on the plate. Slide back into the pan and cook the second side until browned.

Meanwhile, heat the rest of the oil in another pan and stir-fry the peppers, onions and garlic over a high heat until everything is tender and golden. Season well. Keep warm if the potatoes aren't ready yet.

When the potato rosti and vegetables are nearly cooked, bring a pan of water to simmering and poach the eggs lightly. When you are ready to serve, divide the rosti between four plates, top with the pepper mixture and then an egg. Finish with a sprinkling of chilli sauce.

NOTE

✦ *If you want the dish to look prettier – say, for a dinner party – divide the grated potato into four and form into patty shapes before cooking.*

Mushroom and Sweetcorn Sizzle with Thai Flavours

<u>SERVES 4</u>

CALORIES: 128	PROTEIN: MEDIUM
TOTAL FAT: 4.9 g	CARBOHYDRATE: ★★★
SATURATED FAT: 1 g	FIBRE: 3.5 g

MANY Thai dishes are rich in coconut cream or milk which is a very high-fat food. This stir-fry uses Thai flavours but is less fatty.

15 g (½ oz) dried Chinese mushrooms (see Note, below)	150 g (5 oz) pak choi, roughly chopped
1½ tablespoons groundnut oil	100 g (3½ oz) beansprouts
150 g (5 oz) fresh baby sweetcorn	2 teaspoons Thai fish sauce or soy sauce
1 red onion, thinly sliced	juice of 1 lime
1 stalk lemon grass, bruised	salt and black pepper
1 green chilli, de-seeded and sliced	1 tablespoon chopped fresh coriander
300 g (10 oz) shiitake mushrooms, sliced (see Note, below)	

Soak the dried mushrooms in boiling water for 20 minutes, then drain, reserving the water. Heat the oil in a non-stick wok or large frying pan and stir-fry the sweetcorn and onion over a high heat for about 4 minutes or until golden. Add the lemon grass, chilli, dried and fresh mushrooms and pak choi, and stir-fry for 2 minutes. Add the beansprouts, fish or soy sauce, a little of the mushroom soaking water and the lime juice, and stir again. Check the seasoning, remove the lemon grass, and serve sprinkled with coriander.

NOTES AND TIPS
✦ *You can use a mixture of fresh mushrooms if you prefer – say, half shiitake and half less expensive mushrooms. But do try to add some shiitake as they have such a good flavour.*
✦ *Serve with noodles or rice.*

Quick and Easy Vegetable Gratin

<u>SERVES 4</u>

CALORIES: 324	PROTEIN: HIGH
TOTAL FAT: 14 g	CARBOHYDRATE: ★
SATURATED FAT: 4.6 g	FIBRE: 7.4 g

THIS dish is ideal for using up bits and pieces of vegetables left in the fridge, or for raiding the vegetable compartment of the freezer when you're short of ideas.

1 kg (2¼ lb) mixed prepared vegetables, e.g. broccoli, cauliflower, carrots, peas, green beans	1 teaspoon mustard powder
40 g (1½ oz) sunflower margarine	100 g (3½ oz) half-fat mature Cheddar cheese, grated
40 g (1½ oz) plain flour	salt and black pepper
600 ml (1 pint) skimmed milk	

If necessary, cut the vegetables into small chunks or florets. Steam or boil in a very little salted water, adding them to the pan according to the length of cooking time needed, i.e. carrots first, cauliflower and broccoli next, then peas and beans. If mixing fresh and frozen vegetables, cook them in separate pans. Cook them all until they are just tender but still retaining some bite, then drain and tip them into a gratin dish.

Meanwhile, melt the margarine in a saucepan and stir in the flour. Cook, stirring, for 2 minutes. Remove from the heat and slowly add the milk, stirring, until you have a smooth sauce. Return to the heat and bring to the boil, stirring constantly until thick and smooth. Add the mustard and two-thirds of the cheese, and season. Stir again to melt the cheese, then pour over the vegetables. Top with the remaining cheese and grill under a medium-high heat until the top is bubbling and golden.

Tofu and Peanut Stir-Fry

SERVES 4

CALORIES: 212	PROTEIN: HIGH
TOTAL FAT: 15 g	CARBOHYDRATE: ★
SATURATED FAT: 2.5 g	FIBRE: 2.1 g

TOFU, being made from soya beans, is a pulse, though it is hardly recognisable as such in the form of silken tofu, a delicious creamy confection that looks a little like soft cheese. Although it is rarely recommended for use in stir-fries, I find it gives the best texture and flavour (firm tofu can be a bit chalky). Healthwise, tofu is almost beyond reproach as, amongst other things, it is good for the heart, and is anti-cancer and anti-menopausal symptoms.

500 g (18 oz) silken tofu	100 g (3½ oz) bamboo shoots, sliced
1 tablespoon groundnut oil	50 g (2 oz) shelled unsalted dry-roasted peanuts
1 teaspoon grated fresh ginger	1 tablespoon light soy sauce
1 teaspoon chopped fresh chilli	1 tablespoon yellow bean sauce
1 clove garlic, crushed	1 teaspoon chilli sauce
6 cm (1¼ inch) piece cucumber, sliced in half lengthways, de-seeded and cut into batons	2 teaspoons smooth or crunchy peanut butter (unsalted)
100 g (3½ oz) Chinese leaves, sliced	juice of 1 lime

Drain the tofu, pat dry on absorbent kitchen paper and, with a sharp knife, carefully cut into slices. Heat the oil in a non-stick wok or large frying pan and stir-fry the ginger, chilli and garlic for 1 minute. Add the tofu and stir-fry for 1 minute over a high heat, turning gently. Add the cucumber, Chinese leaves, bamboo shoots and peanuts, one after the other, stirring each in well. In a bowl, quickly mix together the three sauces with the peanut butter and lime juice, and add to the stir-fry. Stir for 1–2 minutes, then, when everything is well combined and hot, serve at once.

NOTE

✦ *Serve with some rice or egg thread noodles or Thai fragrant rice.*

Curried Potatoes and Spinach

<u>SERVES 4</u>

CALORIES: 279	PROTEIN: HIGH
TOTAL FAT: 10 g	CARBOHYDRATE: ★★
SATURATED FAT: 2.4 g	FIBRE: 7.3 g

THIS is a simple curry with plenty of yogurt stirred in for a creamy texture and added protein. It is ideal if you have some cooked potatoes you would like to use up.

750 g (26 oz) leaf spinach	600 g (22 oz) potatoes, peeled, cooked and sliced
2 tablespoons corn oil	150 ml (¼ pint) vegetable stock
1 large onion, chopped	salt and black pepper
1 clove garlic, chopped	200 g (7 oz) half-fat Greek yogurt
1 tablespoon garam masala	

Chop the spinach and cook in a covered pan with a very little water until wilted, then drain well. (If using frozen spinach, thaw it, drain well and simmer in a pan with no water, until thoroughly heated through, then drain again.) Heat the oil in a large non-stick frying pan and sauté the onion over a medium heat for 10 minutes or until soft and just turning golden. Add the garlic and garam masala, and stir for a minute or two. Add the potatoes and stock, bring to a simmer and cook, uncovered, for 15 minutes. Season, stir in the spinach and the yogurt, and cook for a minute to heat through.

NOTES AND TIPS
✦ *You can add some parboiled broccoli to this dish if you like.*
✦ *Serve with rice or chapatis.*

Vegetable and Quorn Hotpot

SERVES 4

CALORIES: **267**	PROTEIN: HIGH
TOTAL FAT: **10 g**	CARBOHYDRATE: ★★
SATURATED FAT: **0.9 g**	FIBRE: **9.2 g**

QUORN is related to mushrooms. You can buy ready-to-use chunks in packs in supermarket chilled counters, and it actually is rather nice, as well as being high in protein and low in fat. It is very good at absorbing other flavours, which makes it ideal for casseroles. If you cannot get Quorn, use chunks of textured vegetable protein (TVP).

2 tablespoons olive oil	1 sachet saffron strands
1 large onion, sliced	350 g (12 oz) Quorn chunks
400 g (14 oz) potatoes	150 g (5 oz) spring greens, thinly sliced
2 cloves garlic, chopped	150 g (5 oz) green beans
2 teaspoons Hungarian paprika	1 × 400 g (14 oz) can chopped tomatoes
1 teaspoon ground cumin	150 ml (¼ pint) vegetable stock
1 teaspoon ground coriander	salt and black pepper

Preheat the oven to 170°C/325°F/Gas Mark 3. Heat the oil in a flameproof casserole and sauté the onion for 5–10 minutes or until soft and just turning golden. Meanwhile, peel the potatoes and cut into bite-sized chunks. Add the garlic and spices to the pan and stir, then add the rest of the ingredients, including the potatoes, stir well and bring to a simmer. Cover and cook in the oven for 45 minutes or until everything is tender. Alternatively, if you prefer, continue cooking on the hob but keep at a very low simmer.

NOTE
✦ *Serve with crusty bread or a grain.*

Baked Aubergine Supper

CALORIES: 236	PROTEIN: HIGH
TOTAL FAT: 15.3 g	CARBOHYDRATE: ★★
SATURATED FAT: 4.3 g	FIBRE: 4.6 g

HERE I go again with the aubergines! This very simple dish relies on a rich and tasty tomato sauce, the recipe for which follows.

2 medium aubergines	1 quantity Home-Made Tomato Sauce (see page 107)
2 tablespoons olive oil	4 tablespoons slightly stale breadcrumbs
150 g (5 oz) half-fat mozzarella cheese (in a piece, not grated)	1 tablespoon freshly grated Parmesan cheese

Preheat the oven to 190°C/375°F/Gas Mark 5. Slice the aubergines, brush them with half the oil, and arrange on a baking tray. Bake in the oven for 15 minutes or until they are golden and soft.

Arrange a layer of half the aubergine slices in a gratin dish. Cut the mozzarella into thin slices and use half to top the aubergine slices. Repeat the layers, pour over the tomato sauce and bake in the oven for 30 minutes. Mix the breadcrumbs with the remaining olive oil and the Parmesan, and sprinkle over the top. Return to the oven and cook for a further 15 minutes or until the topping is golden.

NOTE

✦ *Serve with crusty bread and a green salad, which will reduce the fat content of the whole meal to a reasonable level.*

Home-Made Tomato Sauce

SERVES 4

CALORIES: **80**	PROTEIN: MEDIUM
TOTAL FAT: **4.2 g**	CARBOHYDRATE: ★★
SATURATED FAT: **0.5 g**	FIBRE: **1.8 g**

THIS can be used in so many different dishes that you should make up a large batch and freeze the surplus.

I tablespoon olive oil	2 teaspoons sundried tomato paste
I medium onion, finely chopped	I tablespoon lemon juice
I clove garlic, chopped	I teaspoon brown sugar
I × 400 g (14 oz) can chopped Italian tomatoes (best quality)	salt and black pepper
	a little tomato juice or passata
I tablespoon tomato purée	

Heat the oil in a non-stick frying pan and sauté the onion for 5–10 minutes or until soft and transparent. Add the garlic and stir for 1 minute, then add the remaining ingredients (including about 4 tablespoons tomato juice or passata). Stir well and simmer for at least 30 minutes until you have a rich sauce, stirring from time to time. Should the sauce get a little too thick, add more tomato juice or passata and stir. Check the seasoning and use in your recipe, or cool and freeze.

NOTES AND TIPS
✦ *This is a basic tomato sauce. It's best not to add herbs or spices at this stage as your chosen recipe may not require them, or will specify these additions.*
✦ *For tomato and mushroom sauce, add 100 g (3½ oz) small, thinly sliced mushrooms for the last 10 minutes of cooking.*

Mushroom Crêpes

SERVES 4

CALORIES: 334	PROTEIN: HIGH
TOTAL FAT: 14.5 g	CARBOHYDRATE: ★★
SATURATED FAT: 3.5 g	FIBRE: 2.7 g

PANCAKES and crêpes are useful storecupboard standbys (you can get long-life packs) for quick meals as they can easily be filled with a vegetable mornay mixture and topped with grated cheese, or with roast vegetables and then topped with a tomato sauce. Of course, you can make your own pancakes, if you prefer, and freeze them. The Home-Made Pancake recipe that follows produces light and delicious crêpes, also ideal for Shrove Tuesday.

1 tablespoon olive oil	salt and black pepper
1 medium onion, very finely chopped	2 tablespoons chopped fresh coriander or flat-
400 g (14 oz) mixed mushrooms (see Note, below)	leaved parsley
25 g (1 oz) sunflower margarine	8 pancakes, bought ready-made or made using the
25 g (1 oz) plain flour	recipe on page 109
400 ml (14 fl oz) skimmed milk	2 tablespoons freshly grated Parmesan cheese
1 teaspoon mustard powder	

Heat the olive oil in a non-stick frying pan and sauté the onion over a medium heat for 10 minutes or until soft and just turning golden. Add the mushrooms and cook, stirring constantly, for 3–4 minutes. Set the pan aside.

Heat the margarine in a saucepan until melted and bubbling, then add the flour and cook, stirring, for about 2 minutes. Remove from the heat and slowly add the milk, stirring constantly, until you have a smooth sauce. Add the mustard and seasoning. Tip the sauce into the frying pan with the mushrooms, add the coriander or parsley, and stir everything to mix well together. Preheat the oven to 190°C/375°F/Gas Mark 5.

Put one-eighth of the mushroom mixture in the centre of a pancake and roll up or fold. Place in a shallow baking dish in which all the filled pancakes will fit neatly. Continue until all the pancakes are filled and placed in the dish. Sprinkle the cheese over the top and bake in the oven for 15 minutes or until the top is lightly browned.

NOTES AND TIPS

✦ *A good mix of mushrooms for this would be oysters, shiitake and brown caps.*

✦ *Serve with plenty of salad or a selection of vegetables.*

Home-Made Pancakes

SERVES 4 (MAKES 8 PANCAKES)

CALORIES: 157	PROTEIN: HIGH
TOTAL FAT: 4.5 g	CARBOHYDRATE: ★★★
SATURATED FAT: 0.8 g	FIBRE: 0.9 g

110 g (4 oz) plain flour (see Note, below)	250 ml (8 fl oz) skimmed milk
½ teaspoon salt	2 teaspoons sunflower oil
1 medium free-range egg	

Sift the flour and salt together into a mixing bowl. Make a well in the centre and add the egg, beating it into the flour with a balloon whisk and gradually pouring in the milk. Continue beating until you have a smooth batter the consistency of thin cream with countless tiny bubbles on the surface.

Brush the base of a good-quality omelette pan with a very little oil. Heat the pan and, when it is sizzling hot, add one-eighth of the pancake mixture, swirling it around well to coat the base of the pan completely. Cook for 1–2 minutes, then lift the edge of the pancake with a spatula to see when the underside is golden. When it is golden, use the spatula to flip the pancake over, and cook on the other side for just a few seconds. Transfer the pancake from the pan to a warmed plate. Brush the pan with a little more oil and reheat before adding another batch of pancake mixture. Cook as before, and place the second pancake on top of the first with a sheet of baking parchment between them. Continue like this until you have made all the pancakes.

If you are going to freeze the pancakes, cool them, then place them, still flat and separated by parchment, in a large freezer bag. Seal well.

NOTES AND TIPS

✦ *For sweet pancakes (e.g. for serving with lemon juice on Pancake Day), you can add a little caster sugar or ground cinnamon to the mixture.*

✦ *For savoury pancakes, you can vary the type of flour used. Try half plain wheat flour with half buckwheat, or half plain white with half wholemeal flour, or add a tablespoon or two of oatmeal to the flour.*

Vegetable Burgers

CALORIES: 238	PROTEIN: Medium
TOTAL FAT: 5.4 g	CARBOHYDRATE: ★★★
SATURATED FAT: 0.9 g	FIBRE: 5.1 g

IF you have children and fancy your hand at making some home-made vegetable burgers rather than relying on the commercial ones, try these. They are light and not at all like shop-bought ones because you can actually see pieces of real vegetable, and different colours, in the finished burgers.

275 g (9½ oz) leeks, chopped	I medium free-range egg
300 g (10 oz) floury old potatoes	100 g (3½ oz) fresh breadcrumbs
250 g (9 oz) carrots, grated	salt and black pepper
I medium onion, very finely chopped	I tablespoon corn oil
I tablespoon chopped fresh parsley	

Cook the leeks by steaming, microwaving or in a very little lightly salted boiling water until tender. Drain very well and dry further on absorbent kitchen paper. Peel and cube the potatoes and parboil for 3 minutes only. Drain well and leave to cool, then grate them on a coarse grater into a mixing bowl. Add all the other vegetables, including the leeks, with the parsley, egg, breadcrumbs and seasoning. Mix well and shape into eight small burgers, or four huge ones if you prefer. Heat the oil in a large non-stick frying pan and fry the burgers for 3–4 minutes on each side, until golden and completely cooked through.

NOTE
✦ *Serve with home-made parsnip chips and peas or sweetcorn, or with a salad. To make parsnip chips, cut peeled parsnips into chips, spread on a baking tray and brush with oil. Bake in the oven at 200°C/400°F/Gas Mark 6 for 30–40 minutes, turning once.*

CHAPTER NINE

SIDE DISHES AND SALADS

Lots of the recipes in this book are complete meals in themselves, but others benefit from being accompanied by a salad or side dish of some sort, and this chapter contains some very varied ideas.

When choosing a side dish, balance it with the rest of your meal, firstly from a nutritional point of view. For example, if the main part of your meal is relatively high in fat, choose a low-fat side dish; if your main meal is lowish in fibre, choose a high-fibre side dish. And, of course, if your main dish includes, say, tomatoes as a main ingredient, don't choose a side dish which is also strong on tomatoes. Secondly, balance things out so the tastes marry well and the whole meal looks inviting.

If you haven't time to make a side dish from a recipe, don't be afraid to keep things simple. Most dishes are complemented by a simple salad of one or two leaves tossed in a tasty vinaigrette, or by a selection of lightly cooked vegetables, perhaps with a chopped herb garnish.

Many of the side dishes in this chapter can be used as starters (e.g. Potato and Mushroom Medley, page 112; Marinated Courgettes, page 115; Tzatziki, page 119; Avocado Salad, page 120) or as the basis of a more substantial lunch or supper. For example, you could add diced cheese to the Potato and Mushroom Medley; you could add some diced cooked chicken (if you eat poultry) or walnuts to Sautéed Spinach and Pine Nuts (page 114); you could add hard-boiled egg or mixed nuts to the Salad of Artichoke Hearts and Asparagus (page 113); and you could mix some cooked salmon into the Avocado Salad.

Further suggestions for what to team up with the side dishes appear in the notes with each recipe.

Potato and Mushroom Medley

<u>SERVES 4</u>

CALORIES: 124	PROTEIN: LOW
TOTAL FAT: 4.7 g	CARBOHYDRATE: ★★★
SATURATED FAT: 0.8 g	FIBRE: 2.1 g

THIS easy dish makes a good accompaniment for plainly grilled fish or, even better, an omelette.

450 g (1 lb) new potatoes	salt and black pepper
1 tablespoon olive oil	16 stoned black olives, halved
200 g (7 oz) firm mushrooms, sliced	1 tablespoon chopped fresh parsley
1 clove garlic, well crushed	1 tablespoon red wine vinegar

Dice the potatoes if they are large and cook in lightly salted boiling water for about 20 minutes or until tender. Drain. Heat the oil in a non-stick frying pan, add the mushrooms, garlic and seasoning, and stir-fry for 2 minutes. Add the olives, potatoes, parsley and red wine vinegar, and stir gently for a minute or two. Serve warm or cold.

NOTE
✦ *If you are using this dish as a starter, drizzle a little more olive oil and vinegar over the top before serving.*

Salad of Artichoke Hearts and Asparagus

SERVES 4

CALORIES: 116	PROTEIN: HIGH
TOTAL FAT: 8.5 g	CARBOHYDRATE: ★
SATURATED FAT: 0.2 g	FIBRE: 4 g

THIS is a good summer side dish which would go well with plain grilled salmon brochettes, Tangy Cod Fillets (see page 47), or Stir-Fried Peppers with Rosti and Poached Eggs (see page 100).

8 canned or bottled artichoke hearts, drained	4 tablespoons classic French dressing
16 fresh asparagus spears, lightly steamed	4 small spring onions, finely chopped
2 Little Gem lettuces, quartered	2 teaspoons chopped fresh mint

Arrange the artichokes, asparagus and lettuce quarters on serving plates and pour over the dressing. Sprinkle on the onions and mint, and serve.

NOTE
✦ *A few grilled red pepper strips are a nice addition to this salad if it is being served with fish.*

Sautéed Spinach and Pine Nuts

CALORIES: 85	PROTEIN: MEDIUM
TOTAL FAT: 7.5 g	CARBOHYDRATE: ★
SATURATED FAT: 0.7 g	FIBRE: 1.7 g

THIS robust side dish goes well with pulses, white fish, and cheese dishes.

300 g (10 oz) leaf spinach	2 tablespoons pine nuts
1 tablespoon olive oil	salt and black pepper

Put the spinach in a large saucepan with a little water. Cover tightly and cook for a few minutes or until the leaves have wilted. Drain very thoroughly. Heat the oil in a non-stick frying pan, add the pine nuts, and cook, stirring, until they become golden. Add the spinach and stir again, then season and serve.

NOTE

✦ *You could use chopped walnuts or sunflower seeds instead of the pine nuts.*

Marinated Courgettes

SERVES 4

CALORIES: 56	PROTEIN: MEDIUM
TOTAL FAT: 3.2 g	CARBOHYDRATE: ★★
SATURATED FAT: 0.5 g	FIBRE: 1.6 g

THIS is a lovely, tangy late summer salad which goes especially well with fish and with many rice dishes.

2 very fresh medium courgettes (see Note, below)	1 tablespoon olive oil
2 canned or bottled red peppers, well drained and chopped	1 clove garlic, well crushed
1 tablespoon lemon juice	2 teaspoons chopped fresh summer savory or marjoram
1 tablespoon lime juice	salt and black pepper

Top and tail the courgettes and slice them lengthways very thinly indeed. Lay them in a shallow dish with the peppers scattered around. Mix together the citrus juices, oil, garlic, herbs and seasoning, and pour this over the courgettes. Cover and leave in a cool place for up to 12 hours, turning the courgettes in the dressing once or twice, by which time the courgettes will have absorbed some of the dressing and become less crunchy. Serve cold in small dishes.

NOTES AND TIPS

✦ *You could use thinly sliced button mushrooms instead of the red pepper for a change, and you could use fresh peppers if you grill them first.*

✦ *If the courgettes are quite long, slice them on the diagonal so that you get slightly shorter, prettier slices.*

Braised Onions and Tomatoes

CALORIES: 85	PROTEIN: LOW
TOTAL FAT: 3.2 g	CARBOHYDRATE: ★★★
SATURATED FAT: 0.5 g	FIBRE: 1.9 g

THIS is a great winter dish to go with baked fish, eggs, or cheese dishes.

1 tablespoon corn oil	200 ml (7 fl oz) unsweetened apple juice
2 medium onions, cut horizontally into thick slices	salt and black pepper
1 bay leaf	4 medium to large tomatoes, sliced horizontally

Heat the oil in a non-stick frying pan, add the thick onion slices, and cook each side until golden. Add the bay leaf, apple juice and seasoning, bring to a simmer, cover and cook for 30–40 minutes or until the onions are quite soft. Add the slices of tomato to the top of the pan, cover again and cook for a further 15 minutes or until they, too, are soft. Add a little more seasoning to taste and serve hot.

NOTE

✦ *If you have any cider, you could use that instead of the apple juice.*

Pineapple Coleslaw

SERVES 4

CALORIES: 93	PROTEIN: HIGH
TOTAL FAT: 0.7 g	CARBOHYDRATE: ★★★
SATURATED FAT: 0.3 g	FIBRE: 3.4 g

COLESLAW makes a tasty winter salad which goes well with pulses and very many other dishes. This is a twist to the original, adding fibre as well as a great new taste.

200 g (7 oz) white cabbage, shredded	salt and black pepper
I large very fresh carrot, grated	I tablespoon coconut milk
2 spring onions, finely chopped	4 tablespoons natural low-fat bio yogurt
8 pieces no-need-to-soak dried apricot, chopped	
100 g (3½ oz) fresh pineapple chunks in juice, drained (reserving the juice) and chopped	

In a mixing bowl, combine the cabbage, carrot, spring onions, apricot and pineapple pieces. Mix together 1 tablespoon of the pineapple juice with the seasoning, coconut milk and yogurt, beating well to combine. Taste and add a little more pineapple juice if the dressing isn't tangy enough for you. Pour this dressing over the salad and mix well. Serve cold.

NOTES AND TIPS
+ *You can add chopped dessert apple to this recipe if you like, but toss the apple in some pineapple or lemon juice first to prevent discolouration.*
+ *You could use all coconut milk in the dressing, instead of using yogurt, but that will add a lot more fat to the dish.*

Herb Salad with Orange Vinaigrette

CALORIES: 67	PROTEIN: LOW
TOTAL FAT: 6 g	CARBOHYDRATE: ★
SATURATED FAT: 0.9 g	FIBRE: 1.3 g

THIS is another great summer salad which is ideal for livening up rather bland dishes or for kicking your tastebuds into life at the end of a particularly rich meal . . . not that you have many of those, of course . . .

1 head chicory	a few fresh basil leaves
50 g (2 oz) radicchio	2 tablespoons extra-virgin olive oil
1 butterhead, or other mild lettuce	2 tablespoons orange juice
15 g (½ oz) rocket	salt and black pepper
15 g (½ oz) watercress	a few thin orange slices
a few young dandelion leaves (optional)	

Separate the leaves from the chicory, radicchio and lettuce, and wash and dry all the salad leaves. Mix together in a large salad bowl. Mix together the olive oil, orange juice and seasoning, and toss with the salad. Serve the salad straight away, garnished with orange slices.

NOTE

✦ *If you can get them, add some sorrel leaves or lovage. You can also add some thinly sliced peppery radishes to the salad if you like.*

Tzatziki

SERVES 4

CALORIES: **67**	PROTEIN: HIGH
TOTAL FAT: **3.8 g**	CARBOHYDRATE: ★
SATURATED FAT: **2.2 g**	FIBRE: **0.3 g**

THIS is perhaps my favourite side dish of all, combining as it does a sublime amount of garlic with lovely creamy Greek yogurt and delicate, cool cucumber. Perfect for any spicy or rice dish, it also makes a great dip or starter to serve with crudités or slices of pitta bread.

300 g (10 oz) Greek yogurt	2 teaspoons white wine vinegar
3–4 cloves garlic, well crushed	salt and black pepper
6 cm (2½ inch) piece cucumber, finely chopped	

Mix everything together and chill well before serving.

NOTE

✦ *You could use half-fat Greek yogurt or ordinary natural low-fat bio yogurt if you want to cut down the fat content. Perhaps you will make that decision based on how much fat there is in the dish you are serving with the tzatziki.*

Avocado Salad

<u>SERVES 4</u>

CALORIES: 164	PROTEIN: LOW
TOTAL FAT: 16 g	CARBOHYDRATE: ★
SATURATED FAT: 2.1 g	FIBRE: 3.1 g

THERE is something wonderful about a creamy avocado mixed with buttery salad leaves. If you add a few home-made croûtons or crispy fried garlicky breadcrumbs, this turns into an excellent dinner-party starter.

1 butterhead or iceberg lettuce, sliced	3 cm (1¼ inch) piece cucumber, thinly sliced
15 g (½ oz) watercress	1 large ripe avocado
2 good tomatoes, thinly sliced and halved	3 tablespoons classic French dressing
4 spring onions, finely chopped	

Put the lettuce in a serving bowl with the watercress, tomatoes, spring onions and cucumber. Cut the avocado in half, remove the stone and peel the halves. Cut the halves into thin slices, halving again any that are large. Toss the slices into the salad and stir to combine. Add the French dressing, and stir again. If the avocado is nice and ripe, it will mash down a little and form part of the dressing, though most will still be in chunks. Serve immediately.

NOTE

✦ *This goes very well with plainly cooked salmon or trout, with plain baked potatoes, and with garlic bread.*

Spiced Couscous

SERVES 4

CALORIES: 234	PROTEIN: MEDIUM
TOTAL FAT: 1.4 g	CARBOHYDRATE: ★★★
SATURATED FAT: 0.1 g	FIBRE: 1.4 g

SOME people complain that couscous is too bland. Well, here is the answer – a terrific dish to serve with roast vegetables, with curried pulses, with gratins, and much, much more.

400 ml (14 fl oz) vegetable stock	pinch of grated nutmeg
¼ teaspoon each of ground cinnamon, cumin and coriander	2 tablespoons sultanas
	225 g (8 oz) couscous

Put the stock in a saucepan with the spices and sultanas, and bring to the boil. Pour in the couscous, take off the heat, stir and leave to stand for 15 minutes or so. Fluff up the couscous and serve warm with hot dishes, or leave to cool if using in salad dishes, and so on.

CHAPTER TEN

DESSERTS

Can a dessert ever be healthy unless it is a piece of fresh fruit? Oh yes, indeed it can, though you should give some of the calorific disasters such as triple chocolate gâteau, traditional pâtisserie items, suet puddings, and the like, a miss apart from on the rarest of occasions. However, you can still indulge yourself with a regular dessert and not have to feel guilty about it.

If you are just keeping an eye on your waistline, as opposed to actually trying to shed pounds, the pudding possibilities are enormous. After all, many of the more usual dessert ingredients are not, in moderation, unhealthy at all – eggs, milk, flour, even sugar can all fit into an average diet if used with care. Dairy ingredients contain useful protein, vitamins and minerals, and small amounts of sugar are perfectly okay for people in normal health. Add to these wholesome ingredients fresh and dried fruits, juices, nuts, oats and other nutritious goodies and you can see that more puddings than you would believe are, actually, quite good for you. Every single dessert in this chapter will provide nutrients that your body needs, without too many calories. Compared with the desserts you'll find in most cookery books, they are also low in fat, especially saturated fat.

All are also easy, as I have never been the kind of cook who will slave for hours over some fluffy multi-layered concoction which requires a science degree and nerves of steel to execute properly. But if even these are too time-consuming for you, here are some more quick dessert ideas, and they are all fairly guilt-free:

HOT

Fruit compote Slice pears or other firm fruit and simmer in a little sweet wine mixed with orange juice and a spoonful of fructose (see page 131) until the fruit is tender. Serve warm or cold.

Summer berry pancakes   Fill pancakes (see recipe on page 108 or buy ready-made crêpes) with a mixture of summer berries which you have already microwaved or simmered until tender in a very little water with some caster sugar.

Flambéed fruits   Quarter apples, pears and apricots and toss in a little sunflower margarine in a frying pan with orange juice and a little sugar. Add 1 tablespoon brandy when the fruits are tender, and ignite carefully.

Baked bananas   Bake whole bananas in their skins for 20 minutes and serve with Greek yogurt.

Baked peaches   Peel and slice four ripe peaches and bake in a gratin dish topped with dots of sunflower margarine, a few flaked almonds and about 2 tablespoons white wine.

Quick brûlée   Beat together half-fat crème fraîche and Greek yogurt and spoon over fresh fruits in individual heatproof dishes. Cover completely with soft brown sugar and grill until the sugar bubbles.

Easy crumble   Open a couple of cans of fruit in natural juices, e.g. peaches, pears, apricots or pineapple, and put in an ovenproof dish. Top with a crumble made from muesli mixed with a little wholemeal flour, brown sugar and sunflower margarine, and bake until golden.

COLD

Fresh berry sundaes   In sundae glasses, layer low-calorie ice cream with fresh berries and top with a swirl of aerosol cream (there are only a few calories per swirl).

Melon fruit cups   Halve a cantaloupe melon, scoop out most of the flesh and cut into chunks. Mix with raspberries and grapes and serve in the melon halves, topped with a little apple juice and Greek yogurt.

Melon 'Melba'   Slice a ripe melon and arrange on serving plates. Top with a raspberry sauce made by puréeing raspberries in a blender with icing sugar, then sieving to remove the pips.

OPPOSITE Coulibiac Filo Tarts (page 81) served with Marinated Courgettes (page 115)

OVERLEAF Blackberry and Apple Layers (page 131) and Fresh Figs in Red Wine (page 129)

Old–Fashioned Baked Apples

<u>SERVES 4</u>

CALORIES: 104	PROTEIN: LOW
TOTAL FAT: 0.2 g	CARBOHYDRATE: ★★★
SATURATED FAT: TRACE	FIBRE: 2.2 g

WE are lucky enough to have a Bramley apple tree in our garden and every September my children can't get enough of these baked apples, recipe courtesy of my own mother.

4 Bramley cooking apples, or other good cookers	1 tablespoon soft brown sugar
2 tablespoons sultanas	1 tablespoon golden syrup

Preheat the oven to 200°C/400°F/Gas Mark 6. Core the apples and then score a horizontal line through the skin all the way round, about a third of the way down from the top. Place the apples in a baking dish (not too big, but just large enough so that the apples sit about 2 cm (¾ inch) apart). Fill the core spaces with a mixture of the sultanas and sugar. Drizzle the syrup over the top of each apple, and then spoon 4 tablespoons water into the dish around the apples. Bake in the oven for 40–50 minutes, basting at least twice with the syrupy sauce, and stirring a little more water in if the sauce looks like drying out. The apples are ready when they are puffed up like soufflés and, when pierced with a sharp knife, the flesh is as soft as butter all the way through to the centre. Serve immediately, pouring all the caramelised juices from the dish over the apples.

NOTES AND TIPS
+ *Some people say you should add knobs of butter to the apples before cooking but I don't find this necessary. The main thing is to keep basting, and adding more water to the dish if it looks to be drying out. Also, if your oven has 'hot spots', turn the dish around once during cooking as the apples, although needing a high heat to bake properly, will also burn quite easily.*
+ *For a change you could fill the cavities with blackberries instead of sultanas.*
+ *Serve with low-fat custard or half-fat crème fraîche.*

Pear and Plum Pudding

SERVES 4

CALORIES: 231	PROTEIN: MEDIUM
TOTAL FAT: 5 g	CARBOHYDRATE: ★★★
SATURATED FAT: 2.1 g	FIBRE: 3.5 g

THIS is another delicious autumn dessert, and very easy to make.

60g (2½ oz) plain flour	low-fat cooking spray
pinch of salt	6 ripe Victoria plums
40 g (1½ oz) caster sugar	2 ripe dessert pears
2 medium free-range eggs	1 tablespoon lemon juice
250 ml (9 fl oz) skimmed milk	a little icing sugar
50 ml (2 fl oz) half-fat crème fraîche	

Preheat the oven to 200°C/400°F/Gas Mark 6. Sift the flour and salt into a mixing bowl and stir in the sugar. Make a well in the centre and break in the eggs. Beat together the milk and crème fraîche. Using a balloon whisk, combine the eggs and flour, gradually adding the milk mixture until you have a smooth batter. Beat thoroughly and set aside.

Spray a baking dish with low-fat cooking spray. Halve, stone and quarter the plums and arrange them in the dish. Peel, quarter and core the pears, dip them in the lemon juice and add them to the dish. Pour the batter mixture over the fruit and bake in the oven for 45 minutes or until the pudding is risen and golden. Serve immediately, dusted with icing sugar.

NOTES AND TIPS
✦ *Use other fruits if you like – apples, peaches or apricots are fine.*
✦ *Serve with Greek yogurt or extra-thick single cream.*

Mixed Fruits en Papillote

SERVES 4

CALORIES: 100	PROTEIN: LOW
TOTAL FAT: 0.2 g	CARBOHYDRATE: ★★★
SATURATED FAT: 0.1 g	FIBRE: 1.7 g

THIS is a good dessert to pop in the oven towards the end of your main course at a dinner party. It then needs no looking after until serving time, when the wonderful aromas will wake everyone's tastebuds up.

1 large orange	2 teaspoons caster sugar
4 slices fresh pineapple, quartered	1 tablespoon Grand Marnier or other orange-
2 bananas (ripe but not over-ripe)	flavoured liqueur
juice of 1 lime	

Preheat the oven to 190°C/375°F/Gas Mark 5. Wash and dry the orange. Using a parer, remove 2 teaspoons rind from the orange and reserve. Using a knife, peel the orange over a bowl, removing all the pith, and slice the orange into rounds. Remove all pips and reserve any juice that is in the bowl.

Cut four large squares of baking parchment or foil and arrange the orange slices and pineapple pieces in the centre of these. Peel the bananas, slice diagonally and arrange on top of the other fruits, then pour over the reserved orange juice and the lime juice, sprinkle over the sugar and drizzle the liqueur over. Finally, sprinkle the orange rind on top. Close up the parcels securely but loosely, leaving some space around the fruit. Bake in the oven for 10–15 minutes. When serving, put the parcels unopened on to serving plates so that diners can enjoy the delicious aromas that escape from the parcels as they are opened, and no juice is lost.

NOTE
✦ *Serve with half-fat crème fraîche or ice cream.*

Baked Peaches Amaretti

SERVES 4

CALORIES: 199	PROTEIN: LOW
TOTAL FAT: 8 g	CARBOHYDRATE: ★★★
SATURATED FAT: 3.3 g	FIBRE: 2 g

THIS excellent dessert gives the impression that you've gone to some trouble and tastes lovely, but is fairly fail-safe and quick to prepare.

50g (2 oz) Italian amaretti biscuits	yolk of 1 medium free-range egg
20 g (¾ oz) butter, softened	4 perfect peaches (ripe but not over-ripe)
40 g (1½ oz) caster sugar	4 tablespoons dessert wine

Preheat the oven to 180°C/350°F/Gas Mark 4. Roughly crush the biscuits. In a mixing bowl, cream the butter and sugar together until smooth and light, then beat in the egg yolk and the biscuits. Halve and stone the peaches and scoop out a little of the peach flesh from each half. Chop this pulp and mix it into the amaretti mixture, then use the mixture to fill the centres of the peach halves. Place the peaches close together in a suitably sized non-stick baking dish and bake in the oven for 20–30 minutes or until tender. Serve with the dessert wine drizzled over.

NOTE
✦ *Serve with ice cream or a spoonful of Mascarpone cheese.*

Zabaglione with Summer Fruits

SERVES 4

CALORIES: 129	PROTEIN: LOW
TOTAL FAT: 4.2 g	CARBOHYDRATE: ★★
SATURATED FAT: 1.2 g	FIBRE: 0.9 g

ZABAGLIONE is easy to make if you aren't frightened of whisking eggs and sugar over hot water (it rarely fails), but practise once first before you try this out on friends!

175 g (6 oz) mixed summer fruits, e.g. raspberries, strawberries, apricots, nectarines	3 medium free-range egg yolks
50 g (2 oz) caster sugar	4 tablespoons Marsala wine or sweet sherry

Peel and chop the fruits, as necessary, and divide between four stemmed glasses. Sprinkle a little of the sugar over them. In a mixing bowl, beat the egg yolks, pour in the remaining sugar and Marsala or sherry, and mix well. Set the bowl over a pan of simmering water (with the bowl not touching the water) and whisk non-stop with an electric hand-held whisk until the mixture becomes thick. Pour immediately over the fruit, filling each glass to the rim, and serve immediately.

NOTE
✦ *Serve with langues du chats, amaretti biscuits or wafer rolls.*

Fresh Figs in Red Wine

SERVES 4

CALORIES: 95	PROTEIN: Low
TOTAL FAT: 0.3 g	CARBOHYDRATE: ★★★
SATURATED FAT: 0.1 g	FIBRE: 1.7 g

IF you've only ever tried dried figs (not my favourite, either!), you will be amazed at how succulent and delicious a ripe fresh fig can be. Figs are full of vitamins, minerals and fibre, too. If you want to cook them, this is one of the best ways.

8 ripe fresh figs	1 piece lemon rind
150 ml (¼ pint) fruity red wine	1 stick cinnamon
50 g (2 oz) fructose (see page 131)	

Preheat the oven to 180°C/350°F/Gas Mark 4. Halve the figs and place in a small baking dish, cut sides up. In a saucepan, boil the wine with the fructose, lemon rind and cinnamon for a few minutes to reduce slightly. Pour this syrup over the figs, cover, and cook in the oven for 15 minutes (remove the lid halfway through) or until the figs are soft, basting once or twice. Remove the cinnamon stick and lemon rind before serving the figs with the wine syrup spooned over.

NOTE
✦ *Serve warm or cool with half-fat crème fraîche or Greek yogurt.*

Filo Strawberry Cups

SERVES 4

CALORIES: 222	PROTEIN: MEDIUM
TOTAL FAT: 8.8 g	CARBOHYDRATE: ★★★
SATURATED FAT: 5.6 g	FIBRE: 1.7 g

A QUICK and pretty summer dessert which is much lower in fat than a traditional strawberry tart made with shortcrust pastry and crème pâtissière.

4 rectangular sheets filo pastry
(about 100 g/3½ oz)

low-fat cooking spray

60 g (2½ oz) Mascarpone cheese

140 g (5 oz) half-fat Greek yogurt

50 g (2 oz) low-fat custard

1 tablespoon icing sugar, sifted

325 g (11 oz) small fresh strawberries, hulled

1 tablespoon good-quality reduced-sugar
strawberry jam or redcurrant jelly

mint leaves

Preheat the oven to 180°C/350°F/Gas Mark 4. Have ready four non-stick individual flan tins. Spray each filo sheet on both sides with low-fat cooking spray and cut into four squares. Line each tin with four squares of filo, arranging the squares so that the corners form a star shape. Bake in the oven for about 10 minutes or until golden, then leave to cool.

Beat together the Mascarpone, yogurt, custard and most of the icing sugar. When the filo cases are cold, remove them from the tins and fill them with the creamy mixture. Top with the strawberries. Melt the jam or jelly and brush over the top. Sift over the remaining icing sugar and decorate with the mint leaves.

NOTE

✦ *If you like, serve the filo cups with a strawberry or other fruit coulis made by puréeing prepared fruit with icing sugar to taste in a blender, then pressing it through a sieve.*

Blackberry and Apple Layers

SERVES 4

CALORIES: 212	PROTEIN: LOW
TOTAL FAT: 7.8 g	CARBOHYDRATE: ★★★
SATURATED FAT: 2 g	FIBRE: 3.2 g

A QUICK, cold autumn dessert made especially delicious with the addition of a flapjack-like crumble.

1 large Bramley cooking apple	4 tablespoons breadcrumbs
225 g (8 oz) blackberries, washed and dried	3 tablespoons porridge oats
1 tablespoon orange juice	pinch of ground cinnamon
50 g (2 oz) fructose (see Note, below)	100 g (3½ oz) half-fat Greek yogurt
25 g (1 oz) sunflower margarine	

Peel, core and slice the apple into a saucepan, and add all but four of the blackberries. Add the orange juice and 20 g (¾ oz) of the fructose, stir and simmer for a few minutes until the apple has fluffed and the blackberry juice is running clear. Leave to cool.

Melt the sunflower margarine in a non-stick frying pan, add the breadcrumbs and oats, stir well and fry until golden, stirring frequently. Add the remaining fructose and the cinnamon. Leave to cool.

Divide the fruit mixture between four stemmed glasses and cover with a layer of crumble, using half the oat mixture. Add another layer of fruit, using the remainder, and top this with the yogurt. Finish with a final layer of crumble and the reserved blackberries.

NOTE
✦ *Fructose (fruit sugar) is twice as sweet as sugar for the same number of calories, so is worth using occasionally in place of sugar in recipes such as this, when the volume of sugar isn't crucial to the recipe.*

Crunchy Pear Sundaes

CALORIES: 229	PROTEIN: MEDIUM
TOTAL FAT: 5.7 g	CARBOHYDRATE: ★★★
SATURATED FAT: 2.6 g	FIBRE: 1.7 g

THIS is a sublime combination of cream, crunch and fruit; good enough to serve at a dinner party though there's no cooking involved.

1 × 400 g (14 oz) can pears in juice, drained *or* 4 large fresh pears, peeled, cored, sliced, poached and drained	100 g (3½ oz) low-fat fromage frais
	2 individual meringue nests
	8 gingernut biscuits
200 g (7 oz) half-fat Greek yogurt	1 tablespoon amaretto liqueur (optional)
2 teaspoons icing sugar	a few toasted flaked almonds (about 7 g/¼ oz)

Divide half the pear slices between four sundae glasses. Beat together the Greek yogurt, icing sugar and fromage frais. Lightly crush the meringue nests into small pieces. Place the biscuits between sheets of foil and crush lightly with a rolling pin. Mix the meringue and ginger nuts into the yogurt mixture and spoon half over the pears. Drizzle on the amaretto, if using, then put the rest of the pears on top, followed by the remaining yogurt mixture. Decorate with flaked almonds.

NOTE

✦ *You could use peaches, mangoes or nectarines in this recipe instead of pears.*

Peach Melba Meringue Nests

<u>SERVES 4</u>

CALORIES: 200	PROTEIN: LOW
TOTAL FAT: 2.1 g	CARBOHYDRATE: ★★★
SATURATED FAT: 0.5 g	FIBRE: 2.1 g

THE funny thing about meringues is that they are both low in calories and virtually fat free, so they are an ideal ingredient to add a touch of indulgence to a healthy dessert.

150 g (5 oz) raspberries	2 ripe peaches, skinned if preferred
2 teaspoons icing sugar	4 individual meringue nests
1 tablespoon framboise liqueur (optional; see Note, below)	4 scoops low-calorie vanilla ice cream
	1 tablespoon chopped mixed nuts

In an electric blender, purée the raspberries with the icing sugar and liqueur, if using. Press through a sieve to remove the seeds, and chill. Stone and slice the peaches. Put the meringue nests on serving dishes and then top with the ice cream, peach slices and raspberry sauce. Sprinkle chopped nuts on top before serving.

NOTE

✦ *If you are not using the liqueur, add a little peach juice or orange juice to the sauce to thin it.*

INDEX